# A YEAR OF SELF-MOTIVATION FOR WOMEN

# A YEAR OF SELF-MOTIVATION FOR WOMEN

## DAILY INSPIRATION, COURAGE, AND CONFIDENCE

**ASHTON AUGUST**

**ROCKRIDGE PRESS**

Interior and Cover Designer: Linda Kocur
Art Producer: Sara Feinstein
Editor: Sean Newcott
Production Editor: Ellina Litmanovich
Production Manager: Jose Olivera

Illustration used under license from Shutterstock.com. Author photo courtesy of Tabor Aragon (With Love Photo).

Paperback ISBN: 978-1-63807-979-8 | eBook ISBN: 978-1-63807-650-6
R0

To every single inspirational woman in my life who has supported me, believed in me, and, in turn, empowered me to do the same for others.

# Contents

Introduction — viii

JANUARY — 1

FEBRUARY — 19

MARCH — 37

APRIL — 55

MAY — 73

JUNE — 91

JULY — 109

AUGUST — 127

SEPTEMBER — 147

OCTOBER — 165

NOVEMBER — 183

DECEMBER — 201

Resources — 221

References — 222

# Introduction

How we talk *to* ourselves becomes the way we talk *about* ourselves and ultimately becomes the way we *see* ourselves (and, by default, how others see us). As motivational speaker Iyanla Vanzant says, "What you tell yourself about yourself, about your life, about your limitations, you will believe."

My name is Ashton August, and I am thrilled to embark on this yearlong journey with you. As a motivational author, speaker, teacher, and wellness entrepreneur, I believe that cultivating empowering self-talk and a healthy mindset opens the door to living an abundantly fulfilling life!

Our self-talk is important—it is a driving force in our self-confidence and the perpetual narrator that colors our experiences, our mood, our feelings, and our perspective. Self-talk, as well as self-motivation, is all about mindset.

I want to share something with you: *I am the woman of my dreams!* I am rooted in a full state of self-acceptance and the confidence that comes along with it. I share this because through our yearlong journey together, it is my greatest wish that you, too, will step fully into knowing and celebrating that *you are the woman of your dreams.*

As women, we give so much of ourselves, and it's time to courageously give *ourselves* the gift of inspiration, a boost of self-confidence, and a heaping dose of motivation. You've probably heard the saying that strength grows in the moment you think you can't go on, but you keep going anyway. Know this: You are stronger than you even realize.

Self-motivation doesn't need to feel daunting. It isn't a scarcity, nor is it a destination. Self-motivation is a journey. Like a deep well, we can continually draw from and rely on it. And just as a positive mindset can be strengthened like a muscle, so too can our self-motivation—one day and one empowering thought and action at a time.

Self-motivation boils down to mindset. It means loving yourself enough to do the work and release any negative habits or behaviors that are holding you back. It's an inside job.

*The Oxford English Dictionary* defines *confidence* as "a feeling ofself-assurance arising from one's appreciation of one's own abilities or qualities." The fact that you are reading this means you are already on your way.

Treat this book as your daily companion for the next year. Each day, you will find an uplifting affirmation, quote, or practice to inspire, support, and motivate you. Think of it as your daily dose of vitamin C for confidence and vitamin E for empowerment.

You'll emerge feeling unwaveringly confident and self-assured, strong in the face of challenges, and have the courage to show up fully in life and embrace *yourself* as the incredible woman you truly are.

Welcoming this book into your daily life is a statement to and for yourself that you are worth it. Know that by this simple act, you have already set into motion a powerful support system and positive shift in your life.

JANUARY

# 1

*Today, I start my journey of personal empowerment. Every action brings me one step closer to the outcome I envision, and I choose to start now.*

# 2

### PERSONAL CREDO

In Latin, *credo* translates to "I believe." Think of a personal credo as your life's mission statement: What are you passionate about, what's most important to you, what do you believe in, and what are your guiding principles?

Your personal credo is like an internal compass—it can act as a guide when you have several competing priorities, improve your decision-making, and, in so doing, help you reach your goals. Your credo also helps clarify and refine your life path or purpose and will increase your confidence and self-assurance as a result.

Write your personal credo for the year ahead. It should be as clear and specific as possible and answer the main questions. The rest is up to you: You can write your credo in list form or expand it out to a paragraph or a page. Make it your own and revisit it often.

# 3
## JANUARY

*The words I speak are in alignment with what I seek in my life. I commit to consciously choosing intentional and empowering self-talk.*

# 4
## JANUARY

## "Let us make our future now, and let us make our dreams tomorrow's reality."

**—MALALA YOUSAFZAI**

# 5
## JANUARY

*I own my greatness. I stand in my power. I do not dim my light or play small. I know what I want, and I know I am capable of achieving it!*

# 6

## SEVEN DAYS OF INTENTION

Intentions empower our actions. Approaching each day with intention can help you feel motivated, present, and in control. This is the key for a successful week!

To start, write out all seven days of the week (it doesn't matter which day you start on; you'll write one intention per day). Then take an inventory of what you have going on each day, including deadlines, projects, activities, and plans. Now, set a simple intention for each day of the week.

If you have a big presentation on Tuesday, your Monday intention could be focus, confidence, and discipline as you prepare. Girls' night on Saturday? Fun! You might choose to focus on simply enjoying and being present with your friends.

Map out your intentions for the week and start each morning by revisiting and solidifying that intention for the day ahead.

# 7

JANUARY

*I give myself permission to seek progress over perfection. I do not hold myself to unrealistic expectations, and I celebrate my small victories. I calmly approach projects one step at a time.*

# 8

## MINDFUL MOMENTS

We often rush through our days on autopilot, checking off as many to-dos as possible. While there's nothing wrong with being productive, there *is* a way to slow down and be more present.

Whether you're driving your kids to school, cooking dinner, brushing your teeth, or checking email, every moment in your day presents an opportunity to be fully present for it.

Name three routine tasks you'll do today. Then, as you approach each task, challenge yourself to approach it as if for the very first time. For example, when you brush your teeth, notice the feeling of the bristles against each individual tooth. If you drive somewhere, feel the resistance of your foot against the gas pedal. Take a new way home and observe the scenery.

With any task, you can slow down and experience it with mindful presence.

# 9

*I take comfort in knowing that my progress toward my next chapter doesn't need to resemble anyone else's.*

# 10

## JANUARY

"Your mind is a garden. Your thoughts are the seeds. You can choose to grow flowers, or you can choose to grow weeds."

**—ANONYMOUS**

# 11

## JANUARY

*My time is worth protecting. My self-care and soul-care are worth prioritizing. My mind and my body deserve it. When I commit to these things, I am able to give my best.*

# 12

## AUTOCORRECT SELF-JUDGMENT

The opposite of self-judgment is self-acceptance. Through practicing self-love and self-acceptance, we gain more self-assurance.

Today, become acutely aware of any judgmental thoughts you think about yourself. Try not to get down on yourself for having these thoughts. You are human, and we all do it! Anytime a judgmental thought surfaces, simply view it as an opportunity to replace it with an empowering thought. *I never do anything right!* becomes *I am capable and confident, and I always do my best.*

When we can truly love and accept ourselves, we are able to drop the heavy weight of self-criticism and judgment that's been holding us back. When you create a habit of autocorrecting negative thoughts, empowering thoughts will become your new default.

# 13

JANUARY

*I plant seeds in the garden of my mind that feed the vision of where I want my life to go, and every day, I water them with positive thoughts and empowered action.*

# 14

JANUARY

*I am on my own authentic path. My purpose is clear, and I enjoy each step of the journey. Every day brings me closer to what I seek, and I don't rush the process.*

# 15

JANUARY

## CREATE YOUR OWN AFFIRMATION

Affirmations are empowering statements that *affirm* a particular belief, mindset, or action. Affirmations that begin with "I am" statements are powerful tools that help us manifest what we seek.

Here's how to make your own: Start by asking yourself what this affirmation's mission or purpose is for you. What is a current need that this affirmative "I am" statement can support?

Once you've answered these questions, draft your affirmation! It can be simple or more robust, but short enough that you can remember. As long as it feels empowering and resonates with your needs, your affirmation is complete.

Now you're ready to take your affirmation for a spin. Recite it often and be sure to say it with confidence and conviction as if it is already a reality.

## 16
### JANUARY

*I embrace my success. I celebrate everything I have accomplished, and there is so much to be proud of! I am becoming more successful every day.*

## 17
### JANUARY

"Take control of your destiny. Believe in yourself. Ignore those who try to discourage you. Avoid negative sources, people, places, things, and habits.
Don't give up and don't give in."

**—WANDA HOPE CARTER**

# 18

## JANUARY

*I do my best and let go of the rest. I trust that I am enough. I am loved, I am supported, and I am doing a great job!*

# 19

## JANUARY

### CONNECT!

When we feel alone, it's easier to slip into feelings of inadequacy, self-doubt, and negativity. When we feel supported, we feel confident, brave, and more self-assured. As humans, we thrive with connection and a sense of community.

For today's practice, connect with someone in your life. And I'm not talking about sending a message on social media! Instead, use this opportunity to establish a deeper sense of connection. Call or spend time with someone who makes you feel inspired or supported. Write a letter to an old friend you haven't talked to in a while.

The loved ones in our lives show us love, give us support, and make us feel seen and heard. Let them! There's power in being that for someone else also. It's a positive feedback loop—embrace it!

# 20
## JANUARY

---

*I act from a place of integrity, confidence, and empowerment because I believe that how I do anything in life is a direct indication of how I do everything.*

# 21
## JANUARY

---

## "Nourish what makes you feel confident, connected, contented. Opportunity will rise to meet you."

—OPRAH WINFREY

# 22
## JANUARY

*I am equanimous. I am peaceful. I am unwavering in my strength and resilience. I am driven, dedicated, focused, and grounded in my purpose and in who I am.*

# 23
## JANUARY

### WOMEN CELEBRATING WOMEN

There is certainly no shortage of inspirational and influential women in the world and throughout history. For today's practice, celebrate some of these women!

Grab your journal and a pen and number five lines 1 to 5. Then, write down the name of a woman who inspires you on each line. They can be past or present, women you know personally, celebrities, or even fictional characters.

Next, beside each name, note how that woman inspires you. Then, think about each woman's qualities and jot down a quality or qualities both you and this woman share.

The purpose of this exercise is to acknowledge the amazing inspiration that's all around you while also honoring the traits that make *you* an inspiration to others.

## 24
### JANUARY

*Within me resides an infinite supply of ideas, inspiration, and creative potential, and it is from this place that I continually find my strength, confidence, and resilience.*

## 25
### JANUARY

> "Never underestimate the power you hold within, for everyone has an untapped source deep within their soul."

—GERMANY KENT

# 26
## JANUARY

---

*When I recognize a challenge and act courageously from a place of strength and calm, I am able to move past the challenge and learn the lesson it was here to teach me.*

# 27
## JANUARY

---

### GUIDED BOX BREATHING

As a yoga and meditation instructor, I often incorporate box breathing into my classes, and my students love it. I personally practice this simple breathing technique anytime I feel anxious. Box breathing is a potent practice for mental focus, and it can also help relieve stress and anxiety.

Start in a comfortable seated position. Sit up tall and take a breath in through your nose as you lengthen your spine skyward. Exhale through your nose as you relax your shoulders, soften your jaw, and unfurrow your brow.

With your next breath, inhale through your nose for a count of 4. Hold your breath at the top for a count of 4, then slowly exhale for a count of 4, holding your breath out at the bottom for a count of 4. Then repeat this 4-4-4-4 practice for at least four rounds (or you can opt to set a 30- or 60-second timer).

# 28
## JANUARY

—

*I remain focused and present through my intentions, actions, and follow-through. I am clear, consistent, and accountable. This is my commitment to myself and for myself.*

# 29
## JANUARY

—

*I know that the single most important opinion in my life is the one I have about myself. I feel inspired, supported, and fortified in my level of self-confidence.*

# 30
## JANUARY

**INNER CHILD LETTER**

When you picture yourself as a child, what age do you see yourself as? What did you look like? What did you feel like? Whatever image of your younger self surfaced first, stick with that. Now, grab your journal or a piece of stationery and set a timer for 15 minutes.

Write a letter to this version of your younger self. Have a conversation with your inner child: What did you need to hear or know back then? What words of love, encouragement, and support did you need at that time? What motivation or wisdom does your inner child need to hear to encourage your adult self now?

Writing to your younger self can be healing, cathartic, and comforting. It can help you process experiences and move on, as well as pinpoint areas where your past or present self could use more love and support.

# 31
## JANUARY

*I speak with clarity, directness, grace, and a pervading sense of ease. I am capable of speaking my truth from a place of courage and compassion, and I do so regularly.*

# 1

## FEBRUARY

*Every woman who loves and accepts herself fully is a powerful force, and I commit to deeply loving and celebrating me every single day. I am the woman of my dreams!*

# 2

## FEBRUARY

*I am surrounded by incredible opportunities, limitless possibilities, and people who love, support, uplift, and celebrate me. In every aspect of my life, I am living in abundance.*

# 3

## SELF-CARE STAYCATION

When stress creeps in, it can feel like it's taking over. The saying "If you're not managing your stress, your stress is managing you" raises the important question of who is in the driver's seat: you or your stress? Enter: self-care.

Create a self-care routine for the week. Choose one act per day to schedule into your calendar like you would a meeting or appointment. These self-care "appointments" are for you and you alone. Whether it's Monday-evening bath time, Tuesday-morning meditation, Wednesday journaling lunch break, or Friday date night with a candle and your favorite book, create a seven-day customized self-care staycation for yourself and enjoy it!

Establishing a consistent self-care routine is key for managing stress. When we manage our stress, we are more empowered to stay motivated and inspired, which makes us feel more confident. In short, self-care is a shortcut to less stress and more confidence!

# 4

## FEBRUARY

_I attract supportive relationships and exciting opportunities with ease. I remain open to love, abundance, and success in all forms, and I celebrate knowing they are already speeding my way._

# 5

## FEBRUARY

## "Self-care is how you get your power. Self-love is how you keep it."

**—PAULA VICTORIA**

# 6

## FEBRUARY

---

*I operate from the highest frequency of love and appreciation for myself, the life I have created, and for all that I am. I love and accept all parts of me.*

# 7

## FEBRUARY

---

### SELF-LOVE BRAIN DUMP

Grab your journal and pen, set a timer for five minutes, and spend it listing all the things you love about yourself—big or small, internal or external, physical traits or mental strengths, etc. Include any and all of it! What we focus on with feeling grows, so when we take time to authentically reflect on and celebrate what we love about ourselves, our self-love expands as a result.

For some of us, this practice can feel a bit challenging or even self-righteous. If you have these feelings, it's okay. Allow yourself to feel and sit with whatever comes up, and then keep going anyway! I promise that with time (hence the five-minute timer), this practice gets easier and more enjoyable. And, over time, if you keep revisiting either this list you made or the practice itself, your mind will start to automatically search for the good and focus on that.

# 8
## FEBRUARY

*My actions create a positive ripple effect within my community and beyond. From this place, I continuously find the motivation and inspiration to keep going.*

# 9
## FEBRUARY

## "We just need to be kinder to ourselves, truly. If we treated ourselves the way we do our best friend, can you imagine how much better off we would be?"

**—MEGHAN MARKLE**

# 10

FEBRUARY

*When I look in the mirror, I see my power, my potential, and my passion. I am a strong, capable, and confident woman. Confidence looks good on me!*

# 11

FEBRUARY

## MIRROR WORK

Mirror work is a powerful practice that will motivate you, help you connect to yourself, nurture a healthy mindset, and set an empowering tone for your day.

Plant your feet firmly hip-distance apart and bring your hands to your hips. Gaze at your reflection in the mirror and say to yourself, "I am strong, capable, and confident! When I look in the mirror, I see an incredible woman who has accomplished so much." Then, take a moment to lovingly acknowledge these accomplishments: "I love you, [*say your name*], and I am so proud of all your accomplishments."

When we honor ourselves and how far we've come, we tap into a lasting sense of gratitude, confidence, and self-motivation.

# 12

## FEBRUARY

*I lovingly accept myself exactly as I am. My imperfections make me human, and I celebrate my uniqueness. I release the impulse to judge, compare, or speak negatively about myself.*

# 13

## FEBRUARY

*I love myself unconditionally. I am open to both giving and receiving love effortlessly. My heart is filled with love, and I offer that love freely to the people in my life.*

# 14

___

## WRITE YOURSELF A LOVE LETTER

Today, write a love letter to yourself. You can write it in your journal, on your computer, or perhaps on a beautiful piece of stationery. Approach writing this letter as if it's addressed to the person you admire most. Then allow yourself to be fully immersed in all the praise, compliments, admiration, and love you can muster. Put it on the page—to you and from you.

*Dear [your name],*

List what you love about yourself, what you're proud of, and the qualities and traits about you that make you amazing. Sing your own praises! Pat yourself on the back. Toot your own horn. Love on yourself! You deserve it, and even if it seems silly at first, embrace it, knowing this love letter is for your eyes only.

Sign off with a meaningful:

*I love you so much.*

*Love, me*

# 15
### FEBRUARY
—

*When I set strong boundaries, I also set valuable standards of self-worth. This is a statement made loud and clear to myself and everyone around me that my boundaries are nonnegotiable.*

# 16
### FEBRUARY
—

## "Tell your heart that the fear of suffering is worse than the suffering itself. And that no heart has ever suffered when it goes in search of its dreams."

**—PAULO COELHO**

# 17
## FEBRUARY

---

*Live simply, love generously, care deeply, and speak kindly. This is my formula for peace, contentment, and joy. I apply it consistently and relax into the tranquility that follows.*

# 18
## FEBRUARY

---

### PEACEFUL PAUSE

The way we bookend our days matters. It sets the tone for our day ahead. So, today, add a peaceful pause by taking five minutes in bed before you go to sleep or before you get up in the morning (bonus: try both options!) to experience how it feels to be fully physically supported.

You will need four pillows (you can substitute cushions or rolled-up blankets) and will do this lying on your back. Place the first pillow beneath your legs, where your knees bend. Place the second pillow vertically beneath your spine. Then place two pillows beneath your head. Rest one hand over your heart and the other hand on your stomach. Take a deep breath in, and, as you exhale an audible *haaaaaa* sound out of your mouth, allow your entire body to soften and relax fully. Rest here, enjoying this tranquil sensation of being supported.

# 19

## FEBRUARY

*I am worthy of experiencing joy, peace, happiness, love, and contentment, and I do not allow limiting thoughts, beliefs, or people to take these things away from me.*

# 20

## FEBRUARY

> "There is a truth deep down inside of you that has been waiting for you to discover it, and that truth is this: You deserve all good things life has to offer."

**—RHONDA BYRNE**

# 21
## FEBRUARY

—

*Being compassionate and forgiving takes less bandwidth than holding on to anger and resentment. I view compassion and forgiveness as important forms of self-care for my mental and emotional well-being.*

# 22
## FEBRUARY

—

### SKINCARE MEDITATION

Loving the skin you're in takes on a whole new meaning with this skincare meditation that encourages you to approach your existing skincare routine with an added touch of mindfulness.

You will need a facial cleanser, damp washcloth, towel, and moisturizer. If you want to light a candle or diffuse essential oils, please do!

Apply the cleanser to your washcloth and make slow, gentle circles, taking care to cover every inch of your face, neck, and chest. Let it sit as you take three deep breaths. Then, slowly and lovingly, wipe it all off with the washcloth and softly pat your skin dry with your towel. Next, rub a generous amount of moisturizer between two fingertips to warm it up and mindfully apply it to your face, neck, and chest.

## 23
### FEBRUARY

—

*I take time for myself to simply breathe, be still, and enjoy a moment of relaxation when I need it. I deserve to rest, take care of myself, and feel good.*

## 24
### FEBRUARY

—

"You don't have to move mountains. Simply fall in love with life. Be a tornado of happiness, gratitude, and acceptance. You will change the world just by being a warm, kindhearted human being."

**—ANITA KRIZZAN**

# 25
FEBRUARY

*I love myself enough to create positive and empowering new ways of thinking that allow me to reach new heights and greater success. I stay committed to this practice every day.*

# 26
FEBRUARY

## HEART OPENER

Our heart is the energy center for giving and receiving love. Think about your posture in relation to your heart center. Do you tend to hunch and round your shoulders, closing off your heart center? Or do you keep your spine tall, your shoulders back, and your head held high? Today's practice is a gentle heart-opening stance to open your heart center to self-love, activate your capacity to love and be loved, and remain open physically and energetically, literally and metaphorically.

Starting in a seated position, extend your arms in a T shape with your palms facing up toward the ceiling. From here, straighten your spine, and gently lift your gaze and your heart toward where the wall meets the ceiling. Stay here for three deep breaths.

# 27

## FEBRUARY

*I am a creative powerhouse! I love exploring all the dimensions that make me, me.*

# 28

## FEBRUARY

### PROJECT PEACE CORNER

Today, you get to create your very own peace corner! A peace corner is a safe space within your home you can visit anytime you need a moment (or as long as you'd like) of calm. This space can be a corner of your bedroom or closet, or perhaps it's a reading nook or meditation area you've already allocated—anywhere you can make your own sanctuary and be alone.

Now, add touches of calm and elements of peace like candles, incense, or an essential oil diffuser. Perhaps you have a beautiful tapestry or artwork you'd like to hang on the wall, pillows or a meditation cushion to add, or a device to play your favorite calming music. Ideally, it's a place where you can dim the lights or close the curtains—anything that creates an ambience of calm, safety, and peace. Go here often and enjoy it.

# 29

## FEBRUARY

———

*When I think about my beautiful spirit and unique personality, I am filled with pride. Like a fingerprint or a snowflake, I am truly one of a kind.*

MARCH

# 1

MARCH

*As the architect of my life, I actively create my reality through my thoughts, words, and actions. I intentionally choose empowering thoughts and words, and my actions reflect this.*

# 2

MARCH

### BREATHE, MOVE, AFFIRM

When we tap into our breath, we find our courage. When we link breath to motion, we find presence. When we affirm that which we seek to be, we discover our manifesting power. Today, you will combine breathing, movement, and affirmation.

You can do this seated or standing, but, if possible, stand with your feet hip-width apart and planted firmly beneath you in front of a mirror.

For the first few rounds, focus on linking breath to motion. With your inhale, reach your arms overhead. With your exhale, bring your palms together and guide them to your heart center. Repeat this several times. When you're ready, add these affirmations to your breath-to-motion flow (feel free to replace any of the words):

**Inhale:** *I am present.* **Exhale:** *I am in control.*
**Inhale:** *I am safe.* **Exhale:** *I am supported.*

# 3

MARCH

*Everything I do is a reflection of my character, so I always try to do my best. Regardless of the outcome, I rest assured knowing that I gave it my all.*

# 4

MARCH

## "What you tell yourself about yourself, about your life, about your limitations, you will believe."

**—IYANLA VANZANT**

# 5

MARCH

*I have the ability to make a change or start anew at any time. I know that I am in control of my thoughts, feelings, decisions, and actions.*

# 6

MARCH

### THREE TO THE THIRD POWER

What we focus on grows, so when we celebrate our power, we increase it. And when we focus on our strengths, it better enables us to show our power to the world.

Grab your journal and a pen, and, on a fresh page, draw three rows across and three columns down. In each column, list three powerful qualities you have in each of these areas: physical, mental, and professional. Three rows is just the minimum, so if you feel compelled to list more qualities, please do! The same applies if there are more life areas you'd like to include.

The point is for you to reflect on the qualities you possess and to write them down as a way of owning these qualities that embody your power, your strength, and how truly incredible you are! Don't hold back; you're done playing small. Celebrate your strengths and watch them multiply!

# 7

MARCH

—

*When I start having anxious thoughts, I interject with positive "what if" questions like, "What if it works out even better than I expected?"*

# 8

MARCH

—

"Eventually all things fall into place. Until then, laugh at the confusion, live for the moments, and know everything happens for a reason."

**—ALBERT SCHWEITZER**

# 9

MARCH

*I remain open to the flow of my life rather than resisting it.*

# 10

MARCH

## ORGANIZE AND DECLUTTER

Spring brings with it an energy of change and renewal. Spring-cleaning can help us hit a nice reset button for our mindset and in our daily life.

Channeling this spring energy, declutter your living space to feel more organized and in control. Cleansing your physical space of the accumulated clutter and excess that you don't need will, in turn, make you feel more spacious and clear.

Start by thinking about a few areas of your home that are most in need of decluttering. Organize this project by room or area (bedroom closet, living area, kitchen, junk drawer, etc.). Sort through your belongings, and make piles to donate, give away, and throw away. Donating and giving away things you don't need stokes the motivational fire and can make the process feel more rewarding.

The key to this practice is to do it on your own terms so that it feels satisfying, not overwhelming.

# 11
## MARCH

*Like a skillful gardener, I plant and tend to the seeds of my intentions and harvest the fruits of my labor. The landscape of my life is in constant, colorful bloom.*

# 12
## MARCH

### GO BEYOND COMFORT

Today is about exploring your boundaries and challenging your perceived limitations in a safe, controlled way. While I won't ask you to jump out of an airplane (unless that speaks to you), I will challenge you to try something you feel intimidated by. For example, I have historically shied away from most water sports, so when I mustered up the courage to try wake surfing, I was shocked to discover how much of an enjoyable, rewarding, and self-affirming experience it was!

Is there an area in your life where you've developed a perception of limitation that you'd like to examine or challenge? Grab your journal and write down your reflections. How do you currently feel stifled, where in your life are you ready to push through, and what can you do to break down this perception of limitation to create one that's more expansive and in alignment with your goals?

# 13
MARCH

———

*I embrace my journey. I trust the process and enjoy the natural progression of my life. I indulge in the peace, joy, and gratitude that follow.*

# 14
MARCH

———

*I proudly live my life with integrity. I make decisions with confidence and self-assurance. I know I can rely on my deep well of inner strength to carry me through.*

# 15
## MARCH

---

### EAT THE FROG

Don't worry—you will not be eating any actual frogs today. "Eating the frog" is my favorite morning productivity hack, originally coined by Brian Tracy in *Eat That Frog!*

This game-changing approach motivates you to tackle your biggest, most daunting task of the day first. That way, you get it done, enjoy the sense of relief and accomplishment that follows, and start your day on a productive note.

We've all had a big project or deadline looming over us that we dread and procrastinate starting until inevitably the deadline arrives, and we frantically rush to get it done. Not a great feeling! When we take control and eat the proverbial frog, we can give it our very best and check off a major to-do. Now *that* feels great! I've adopted this hack in running my business, in my personal life, and even writing this book.

What frog will *you* eat today?

# 16

## MARCH

*I pause often to admire life's incredible beauty, the endless stream of inspiration that surrounds me, and all the things that contribute to making my existence so rewarding.*

# 17

## MARCH

## "If your actions create a legacy that inspires others to dream more, learn more, do more, and become more, then you are an excellent leader."

**—DOLLY PARTON**

# 18
## MARCH
---

*I define exactly what it is that I want in my life, and I say no to anything that is not in alignment with this definition.*

# 19
## MARCH
---

### LUNCH BOX LOVE NOTES

When I was young, my mom used to leave me positive, encouraging notes in my lunch box. I adopted this practice for myself as I got older, and I still leave myself notes in my planner or on my computer. Taking small affirmative steps like this to keep ourselves feeling encouraged can go a long way!

Write yourself at least three notes today. They can be simple statements, like "You are going to have an amazing day," or reminders, like "You are fearless!" You can also make them more customized: "You approach challenges with grace and ease" or "I am so proud of everything you've accomplished this week."

Place your notes strategically in your planner or lunch box, on your computer screen, or on your pillow to find later, and notice how you feel when you see them.

# 20

MARCH

---

*I do my best to not take anything personally. Even when it seems personal, it's most likely not about me. I can never truly know what someone else is going through.*

# 21

MARCH

---

*I acknowledge my need for connection as a means to feel loved, supported, and uplifted by a sense of community. I nourish this need by connecting with my loved ones often.*

# 22

## MARCH

### TIME TO GET CREATIVE

Creativity fosters confidence, so today's practice is all about tapping into your creative side. This can take any form that you'd like it to!

If you love to paint, grab your paintbrush and canvas. If you love to write or draw, grab your pen and notebook. If dancing is your favorite expressive outlet, turn on your go-to song or playlist and have a dance party.

Maybe you're more of a DIYer or arts-and-crafts gal. Perhaps you've had a scrapbooking or vision-boarding project you've been wanting to do. Or maybe you will get creative in the kitchen by trying a new recipe. You can even get creative in your love life by finding a new way to show your significant other that you care.

When you give yourself the opportunity to be creative, you're reminded of how imaginative, resourceful, and original you can be.

# 23

## MARCH

*I feel best when I focus on the positive. It's not about avoiding the negative; it's about choosing to focus on the good things in my life.*

## 24
MARCH

"Joy is not the negation of pain, but rather acknowledging the presence of pain and feeling happiness in spite of it."

—LUPITA NYONG'O

## 25
MARCH

*I listen to and am deeply connected to my internal compass—the gateway to my intuition and wisdom. Here, I find the answers and the solutions I seek.*

# 26
MARCH

## FIND YOUR IDEAL REALM

If anything were possible, what would your ideal realm look like? Do you land your dream job? Do you have more discipline or focus? Do you spend more time doing what matters to you? Or maybe your ideal realm is *feelings* based—one where you don't expend so much energy worrying or doubting.

Grab your journal and describe your ideal realm in detail. Once you're done, it's time to reverse engineer—from the end to the beginning. In other words, map out the realistic steps you need to take to arrive at your ideal realm in backward order.

If, in your ideal realm, you have your dream job, what would need to happen (a job offer, an interview, applying for the job, etc.)? Do the same reverse-engineering process for anything you seek from your ideal realm. Use a simple outline format, Venn diagram, bubble chart, or whatever works best for your brain.

# 27
MARCH

*I am present. I am grounded. I am grateful. When I focus on these qualities, I am reminded of my power. When I focus on my power, I step into my confidence.*

## 28
MARCH

———

"But don't ever underestimate the impact you can have, because history has shown us that courage can be contagious and hope can take on a life of its own."

**—MICHELLE OBAMA**

## 29
MARCH

———

*All my emotions are valid. I allow myself to feel whatever emotions arise in this moment. My heart, mind, and spirit are in alignment when I am present with my feelings.*

# 30

## MARCH

### HYDRATION CHALLENGE!

Hydration is a key factor in overall wellness. From increasing energy levels to improving brain function and flushing out toxins, drinking water is a hack for physical *and* mental fortitude.

While daily hydration is not a one-size-fits-all approach, an easy rule of thumb is to drink half your body weight in ounces of water each day. For example, if you weigh 150 pounds, try to drink 75 ounces of water (or roughly 9½ cups). The foods you eat and other liquids you drink add several more cups' worth of hydration.

Try this today! It may help to keep a big reusable water bottle with you throughout your day to establish and support your hydration habit. Bonus: Spruce up your water by infusing it with sliced cucumbers, watermelon, basil, or other fruits and herbs. Or you can add a dash of sea salt with a squeeze of lemon for natural electrolytes.

# 31

## MARCH

*Every day, I take time to exercise, breathe deeply, take mental breaks, and engage in self-reflection to recharge, de-stress, and maintain balance in my life.*

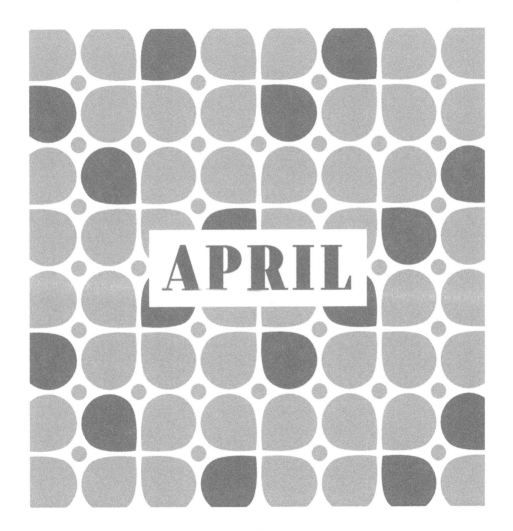

APRIL

# 1

## APRIL

—

*Life doesn't happen to me—it happens for me.*

# 2

## APRIL

—

### TECH DETOX

Nothing throws off our focus like our devices. Most adults spend hours on their phones every day, and that doesn't include time on all the other devices (computer, tablets, TV, etc.). The average millennial, for example, will spend *34 years of their life* on a device. Whoa!

A tech detox can be customized to fit your needs and lifestyle, but here's a simple structure: Schedule time to unplug (8 p.m. to 8 a.m., for example), limit your time on social media (e.g., 30 minutes per day or only check it once a day), and designate "tech-free zones" like your bedroom or backyard. If you can, turn off notifications and keep your phone on silent or vibrate to reduce the number of pings and beeps.

We can't escape technology, but we can certainly establish boundaries around it. And when we do, our mental health, focus and productivity, and overall wellness improve.

# 3

APRIL

*I schedule time for myself just like I schedule important appointments. I make myself a priority and know that, when I do, I replenish my physical, mental, and emotional health.*

# 4

APRIL

"Don't let anyone rob you of your imagination, your creativity, or your curiosity. It's your place in the world; it's your life. Go on and do all you can with it and make it the life you want to live."

**-MAE JEMISON**

# 5

APR I L

---

*I am meant to grow and evolve. Every step forward and every challenge or mis-take are simply here to guide me in my personal growth.*

# 6

APR I L

---

## RITUALIZE YOUR ROUTINE

Routines are instrumental constructs that help us live productively and intentionally. While routines are important, rituals are where routines go to find deeper meaning. Rituals heighten the sense of significance, joy, and intention; they create a deeper level of awareness around the act you perform.

Examine your existing routine. Your routine may be as simple as waking up at 7 a.m., drinking a glass of water, completing your skincare regimen, and reading for 15 minutes before going to work. Your routine may be more extensive.

Break down your routine into individual steps. Choose one step to add a layer of ritual to. How will you *ritualize* that step? For example, as you drink your glass of water, focus on the gratitude you have for it. Or light a candle to signal the start of your skincare routine.

Now, enact your new ritualized routine and enjoy!

# 7

APRIL

―――

*I practice self-love and soul-care regularly. This is a statement of my self-worth to myself and others, and it gives other women permission to do the same.*

# 8

APRIL

―――

"When I dare to be powerful—to use my strength in the service of my vision—then it becomes less and less important whether I am afraid."

—AUDRE LORDE

# 9

APRIL

*When I walk into a room, my energy and my self-assurance introduce me.*

# 10

APRIL

## TALLY YOUR ACHIEVEMENTS

We have all accomplished things in our lives for us to be proud of. When we think about the people who inspire us, it's easy to name *their* accomplishments. Yet it's not always as easy to do this for ourselves.

So, tally up all your incredible achievements that deserve to be celebrated! Writing your résumé is a similar practice of listing your accolades and accomplishments, so channel that energy. Grab your journal and a pen, and start by listing five of your achievements—big or small, personal or professional, or whatever comes to mind. You can stop at five, but if this gets your juices flowing, keep adding your achievements to the list!

Your ongoing assignment (yes, you have homework!) is to continue reflecting on your accomplishments and create a daily habit of celebrating all the incredible things you do! YOU are an amazing accomplishment. Don't ever lose sight of that.

# 11

## APRIL

*I don't shy away from going for what I want, no matter how intimidating or seemingly impossible. Courage and confidence create more courage and confidence.*

# 12

## APRIL

### WOMEN'S CIRCLE

Sometimes in life, it can feel like we're on our own island. Women's circles are a safe space and create a strong support system. They give us a sense of belonging and are a wonderful way to connect and bond with other like-minded women. Personally, my involvement in a women's circle has been revolutionary for my mental health and sense of feeling accepted and supported.

Women's circles, whether virtual or in person, are a safe space and create a strong support system. They can be held weekly or monthly or however often serves the group.

Make a list of women you'd like to create a women's circle with. Then send these women an invite. Together, decide on the frequency and setting, along with the theme, purpose, and focus of your group to form your own supportive and rewarding women's circle.

# 13
APRIL

*When I look back on how far I've come, I realize how amazing this journey has been. When I visualize my future, I know it will only get better from here.*

# 14
APRIL

*Self-talk is a driving force in my self-image. How I talk to myself becomes the way I talk about myself and ultimately becomes the way I see myself.*

# 15
APRIL

*I rewrite the parts of my story that no longer fit my current narrative. It is never too late to make a change, and every positive shift arrives on time.*

# 16
APRIL

---

## "Fall seven times, stand up eight."

**—JAPANESE PROVERB**

# 17
APRIL

---

*If I fall, I get back up. If I waver, my perseverance moves me forward. When I trust in my own capabilities, I unlock an inner fortitude that carries me through anything.*

# 18
## APRIL

### CORE ENGAGEMENT

The abdominal region—the core of our body—is our center of power and strength; it is where courage resides and intuition speaks. To create a physical, palpable connection to your core, it helps to understand and practice abdominal engagement.

Sitting tall in a comfortable chair, gently scoop your pelvis forward as you press your navel in toward your spine. Compress your lower ribs toward your hips to create a light "constant crunch" sensation. Maintain your core muscle engagement by holding the scoop, press, and compress combination for several breaths.

You can apply this simple mind-body connection technique during your physical activities, at your desk, or in your car. It is a quick and core-strengthening way to feel your power anytime.

# 19
## APRIL

*I am my own hero. Turning the page, moving forward, being open to new experiences, and trying different things takes courage. I believe that I can, and so I will!*

# 20
## APRIL

"Owning our story and loving ourselves through that process is the bravest thing that we will ever do."

**—BRENÉ BROWN**

# 21
## APRIL

*Life isn't about avoiding the inevitable challenges that arise; it's about facing them with perseverance and a sense of humor.*

# 22
## APRIL

### EXERCISE YOUR NO MUSCLE

One of my favorite motivational authors, Iyanla Vanzant, popularized the concept of "exercising your no muscle"—being able to say no when we need to establish healthy boundaries *and* affirm our self-worth. This doesn't mean saying "I'm so sorry, but I can't and here's why." This is an empowered, unapologetic *no* without needing to explain yourself. As Iyanla says, it's all about standing firmly *in* your yes and *for* your no.

Think about a key area in your life where you want to strengthen your no muscle. Whether it's saying no to social invites when you're feeling overwhelmed, saying no to a colleague who constantly asks you for favors, or saying no to an opportunity that's not for you, reflect on where you can apply this in your life.

What action step can you take today to start exercising this particular no muscle? Do something that affirms this new boundary.

# 23
## APRIL

*When it comes to my nonnegotiables, I do not compromise. I stand firm in my values, needs, and self-worth, and I set a powerful example for others to follow.*

# 24

"When one door of happiness closes, another opens; but often we look so long at the closed door that we do not see the one which has been opened for us."

**—HELEN KELLER**

# 25

APRIL

*I view my life like a photographer views their art form. I focus my lens on the beauty all around me, and when things aren't working out, I simply try another angle!*

# 26

APRIL

---

### BE THE GRAPE

In *A Complaint Free World*, author Will Bowen eloquently conveys how we lead best by example. He writes, "In a vineyard, one grape will begin to ripen and in so doing will send out a vibration, an enzyme, a fragrance, or an energy field of some kind that is picked up by the other grapes. This one grape signals the other grapes that it is time to change, to ripen."

In the simple yet powerful act of living authentically, you inspire and elevate the consciousness of everyone around you. By empowering yourself to fulfill your dreams, you inspire others to go and do the same.

What standards do you hold high and to what effect? Grab your journal and list five ways in which *you* are the grape.

# 27

APRIL

---

*I attract what I emit. Thus, I emit positivity and confidence, because I know I am a beacon for attracting more of the same.*

# 28
APRIL

## RELEASE FALSE NOTIONS

Many of us live under the shadow of who we (or others) *think* we are supposed to be.

For years, I was consumed with impressing my grandfather. He graduated early from MIT with his master's degree, and though he always supported me in whatever I did, I adopted a false belief that I needed to do certain things by a certain age to earn his approval. Spoiler alert: Those self-imposed beliefs pushed me to do things I later regretted, like graduate high school and my own master's program early just to prove I could instead of enjoying my time.

Releasing who we thought we were supposed to be so we can embrace who we really are is liberating! Grab your journal and reflect on any beliefs or expectations you have about who you *think* you're supposed to be that are stopping you from embracing and enjoying who you really are.

# 29

## MAKE IT RAIN

Created by meditation and mindfulness teacher Michele McDonald, RAIN is a mindfulness tool for increasing your self-awareness. RAIN stands for:

1. Recognize
2. Acknowledge, Accept, Allow
3. Investigate
4. Nonattachment/Natural Awareness

It starts with *recognizing* what is going on with the situation at hand as well as how you respond to it. The second step is to *acknowledge, accept,* and *allow* the situation to simply be without the impulse to judge, label, avoid, or suppress it.

Next, *investigate* it with questions like "Why am I feeling this way?" or "What do I need right now?" Finally, relax into a state of nonattachment and natural awareness where you are reminded that your thoughts and emotions do not define you.

RAIN is particularly useful during challenging situations, since it helps us remove the emotional *reaction* and, with practice, replace it with a mindful *response*. If you are faced with a challenge today, make it RAIN.

# 30
## APRIL

—

*Time is my asset, and I always have enough. I am in tune with myself and my needs to honestly assess when I need rest versus when I'm ready to act.*

MAY

## 1

MAY

*I expect good things, I remain open to good things, I attract good things, and I deserve all the good I can imagine! Life is so incredibly good.*

## 2

MAY

**SCRIPTING SESSION**

Scripting is a simple, fun, and *very* potent way to pull your desired reality into *actual* reality. Part journaling, part narration, and part affirmation, this is where your deepest desires take center stage as you write about what you want yourself and your life to become.

Start by choosing a goal you want to focus on today. Let's say you want to be more self-assured in your daily interactions. Grab your journal and begin to script out that desired reality—in present tense. Here's an example: "Wow, I'm impressed by the way you move through interactions. Each time you speak, you embody confidence. You hold your head high and are so sure of yourself. You approach difficult conversations with such grace and composure."

Now it's your turn! Cast aside any doubts, trust in this practice, and enjoy the process.

# 3
MAY

---

*My voice is important. My thoughts and opinions are worthy of being heard, so I speak with clarity and confidence. People value my mind, my work, and my time.*

# 4
MAY

---

## "If you can dance and be free and not embarrassed, you can rule the world."

**—AMY POEHLER**

**5**

MAY

---

*I will become more successful in life by thinking, believing, and living as if I already am.*

**6**

MAY

---

### VISUALIZE TO MATERIALIZE

Visualization is a mental practice that can increase confidence and motivation. Vision boards are where the power of visualization joins forces with a fun arts-and-crafts project. The process of creating a vision board helps solidify what you want to create or achieve. The result? A visual guide that reminds you of your goals.

Vision boards can represent all the things you want to do, experience, and accomplish. They can also represent how you want to feel and the relationships you want to have. A vision board can include words and/or images. Many people enjoy the tactile experience of assembling them in a visual collage, but others prefer a digital alternative. There is no right or wrong, as long as you're choosing the images and words that make your soul sing and that encapsulate your vision.

Get started on your vision board today!

# 7
### MAY

---

*I consciously and consistently fill my mind with empowering thoughts that are positive, uplifting, and meaningful. My time is too precious to focus on anything less.*

# 8
### MAY

---

"You gain strength, courage, and confidence by every experience in which you really stop to look fear in the face. You must do the thing you think you cannot do."

**—ELEANOR ROOSEVELT**

# 9

## MAY

*I visualize the life I want to lead and trust that I am a powerful creator in manifesting it for myself each and every day. This is a process I enjoy!*

# 10

## MAY

### WONDER WOMAN STANCE

Postural feedback, or "power posing" as Amy Cuddy called it in her popular TED Talk, is the connection between how our posture and body language influence how we feel about ourselves. When we stand tall and take up space, we feel more confident and empowered. In contrast, when we shrink ourselves in a low-power pose (arms crossed, spine hunched, or shoulders rounded), we tend to feel less self-assured.

Find your high-power stance in front of a mirror. Like Wonder Woman would, stand up tall and proud, spread your feet hip-width distance apart, place your hands on your hips, and gaze powerfully at your own reflection. Stay here for a few moments, soaking in your self-generated sense of empowerment.

This stance is helpful if you're feeling nervous, anxious, or overwhelmed. Plus, it reminds you that you can be your own superhero.

## 11
### MAY

---

*Like a tall and majestic tree, I am rooted in my beliefs and stand strongly in my foundation. My self-love is the water that fortifies my foundation and grows my roots deeper.*

## 12
### MAY

---

*I am prosperous, I am limitless, und I am in charge of my success. From my ideas to my talents, I have so much to offer. I am an asset!*

# 13

## PROGRESS OVER PERFECTION

A realistic approach to life is to focus on progress and improvement rather than on perfection. You stop seeking the "final destination" of perfection, and instead focus on actionable steps. You set yourself up for victory, not defeat. When we hold tightly to the notion that something must be perfect, the pressure can be debilitating. When I first heard the saying, "Progress over perfection," I instantly felt liberated from my perfectionist tendencies.

Reflect on where you can replace perfection with progress in your own life. Is there an area of your life where you might be too hard on yourself? Do you recognize any tendencies of perfectionism that detract from your forward movement?

When we release the need to perfect something, we release ourselves from the illusion of perfection. We relax into the peace of progress and accept that this is truly enough. Deep sigh—doesn't that feel nice?

## 14
MAY

---

*There is no need to people please. The people who matter accept me as I am. I establish boundaries that nourish my well-being, and I say no when I need to.*

## 15
MAY

---

"Whatever anybody says or does, assume positive intent. You will be amazed at how your whole approach to a person or problem becomes very different."

—INDRA NOOYI

# 16
## MAY

*I acknowledge and celebrate my achievements and know that honoring all I do is just as important as taking breaks, resting, and spending time to simply be.*

# 17
## MAY

### SELF-MASSAGE

Everyone holds mental or emotional tension somewhere in their physical body. Self-massage can help release physical tension, which can then decrease mental or emotional tension. Bonus: You'll gain a valuable tool for self-soothing that you can use anytime.

Find a comfortable seat. Scan your body and notice where you're holding tension (or where you usually hold tension). Slowly massage that area with one or both hands. As you do this self-massage, breathe deeply, relax, and enjoy.

People often hold tension in their jaw and/or brow. If you clench your jaw, make a peace sign with your fingers, and gently massage where the upper and lower jawbones connect in small circular motions. If you furrow your brow, use the tips of your index fingers to trace the arch of your eyebrows with moderate firmness, and then massage your temples in circular motions.

# 18
## MAY

*I stand resolute in my decisions and do not doubt or second-guess myself. I am confident in who I am. I trust my abilities, my wisdom, my experience, and myself!*

# 19
## MAY

## "Have faith in your skills. Doubt kills more dreams than failure ever will."

**—SUZY KASSEM**

# 20
## MAY

*I hold my head high. I am proud of myself and love everything that I am. Within me dwells a remarkable radiance that nothing outside me can diminish.*

# 21
## MAY

### AWARENESS AUDIT

Thoughts create reality, so our thoughts greatly impact our lives. You are the architect of your life, and your thoughts actively build that life! There's no room for limiting thoughts in the empowered reality you're constructing. If there's an area of your life where you want to make a change, it all starts with the quality of your thoughts.

This audit will help you replace limiting thoughts with empowering thoughts. The "I could never do that" becomes "I can and I will!" Grab your journal and list three negative thoughts you tend to think. Then, next to each limiting thought, write an empowering thought to replace it.

This final step is an important one: Read both thoughts again, then cross out the limiting one to visually and literally symbolize you moving beyond limiting thoughts to a more fortified mindset.

# 22
## MAY

*As I breathe in, I visualize an even more inspired, confident, and empowered me. As I breathe out, I allow anything opposing these qualities to leave my mind.*

# 23

"If you are impeccable with your word, if you don't take anything personally, if you don't make assumptions, if you always do your best, then you are going to have a beautiful life."

—DON MIGUEL RUIZ

# 24

*I expect success and I embody success. I expect joy and I embody joy. I expect and embody good health, wealth, passion, and limitless potential. And so it shall be!*

# 25
## MAY

---

**FLIP YOUR PERSPECTIVE**

Inversions are postures that bring the head below the heart. This increases blood flow to the brain, which improves focus and circulation and provides a mental and physical energy boost.

A standing forward fold is a gentle inversion. This pose is a great way to stretch your hamstrings, release tension, and lengthen the spine (which feels amazing after long periods of sitting). In addition, the forward fold helps flip your perspective, literally, and that's where today's practice comes in!

Standing with your feet three feet apart and a slight bend in your knees, fold your torso forward toward the ground. Grasp your opposite forearms or elbows and gently sway from side to side. Relax your neck and let your head hang heavy. Stay here for 60 seconds (or longer if you wish!), breathing deeply. When you finish, take a moment to notice any physical or mental shifts that may have occurred.

# 26
## MAY

---

*Letting go creates space. Moving on opens the door to new possibilities. When I let go and move on, I get stronger. It isn't always easy, but it's always worth it.*

# 27
## MAY

"I also think you should embrace what you don't know, especially in the beginning, because what you don't know can become your greatest asset. It ensures that you will absolutely be doing things different from everybody else."

—SARA BLAKELY

# 28
## MAY

*I live out my purpose in all areas of my life, which gives it meaning and makes each experience fulfilling. Enjoyment and pleasure come easily to me, and I savor every moment.*

# 29
## MAY

---

### END-OF-DAY MAPPING

In the evening, take some time for reflection. Grab your journal and consider the following:

- What was today's biggest win?
- What was today's highlight(s)?
- Did you face any challenges?
- Did you learn any takeaways or lessons?

You can answer in a few words or a full page—the point is to reflect! Next, answer the following:

- What are three to-dos you want to accomplish tomorrow?

Pick one big yet manageable to-do and a few smaller but necessary to-dos and add them to your planner. This sets your tomorrow up for success. Ask yourself what you need to focus on to stay on track, and figure out how to put those things in place. The final step is to map out any goals or intentions you have for the rest of the week. This end-of-day practice helps you have a restful evening and peace of mind knowing that a productive day ahead awaits.

# 30
## MAY
---

*Being emotionally healthy and resilient takes work and requires a strong dedication to myself and my self-worth. I love myself, I am worth it, and I am committed!*

# 31
## MAY
---

*I nurture the relationships in my life that are healthy, supportive, and fill me up. I respect myself enough to walk away from any relationship that is detrimental to my well-being.*

JUNE

# 1

JUNE

---

*I don't have to do anything. I get to do it! My positive mindset and attitude can turn around any situation, and so I choose to approach everything this way.*

# 2

JUNE

---

*I am the woman of my dreams. I view my life through her eyes. I make decisions and act with her in mind. I love every part of the woman I am.*

# 3

## DATE NIGHT

Get ready for a hot date—with yourself! A big aspect of cultivating confidence is not just being comfortable on your own but also *enjoying* your time alone.

The best part about having date night (or day) with yourself is that you can do whatever your heart desires! Feel like movie night with wine and popcorn? Cue it up! Craving dinner at your favorite restaurant? Make a reservation for your party of one. Take yourself out for a beverage at your favorite coffee shop or make yourself a picnic lunch and enjoy it at the park. Is there an exhibit at the museum you've been wanting to see? A hiking trail you've been wanting to explore?

The choice is yours, so whether you opt for a quick coffee or make it a full-day affair, soak up every single moment of your quality *you* time!

# 4

*I fill my own cup so that I can give the world my very best. I commit to putting myself first so I can give 100 percent to everything I do.*

# 5
### JUNE

"Don't limit yourself. Many people limit themselves to what they think they can do. You can go as far as your mind lets you. What you believe, remember, you can achieve."

**—MARY KAY ASH**

# 6
### JUNE

*Mindset is everything! What I think controls how I act. How I act is how the world receives me. The way I view the world is how the world views me.*

# 7

## INNER-STRENGTH GUIDED MEDITATION

Set aside some time today to enjoy this meditation.

1. Sit comfortably. Close or soften your eyes and breathe through your nose.
2. Place one hand on your heart; the other on your stomach. Allow your body to relax and your mind to slow. Scan your body with awareness.
3. Starting at your feet, reflect on how far they've carried you.
4. Feel gratitude for your ankles, calves, and knees and all the places they've taken you.
5. Acknowledge the power in your thighs and glutes.
6. At your hips and pelvis, take a moment to honor this sacred space of creation.
7. Perceive the power of your core, your heart, and all your organs.
8. Focus on your throat, the center of communication, and finally on your eyes, mouth, and brain, where perception and expression form.
9. Now focus on your whole body and sit with this awareness, feeling your inner strength.

# 8
## JUNE

*I trust and listen to my intuition. When I stop listening to the outside world's chatter, I tap into my inner guidance and find the answers and resolution I seek.*

# 9
## JUNE

## "Dream with ambition, lead with conviction, and see yourself in a way that others may not."

**—KAMALA HARRIS**

# 10
## JUNE

*I can be mindful even when my mind is full. I trust myself and my abilities. Within me resides an infinite supply of wisdom, strength, love, and talent.*

# 11
JUNE

## EARTHING

Earthing, also referred to as "grounding," is the simple practice of sitting, standing, or walking barefoot on the earth as a way of connecting to nature and its many healing benefits. Physically connecting your body to the Earth's surface electrons offers a range of benefits for your overall wellness.

Try earthing for yourself today! Grass, dirt, sand, or even concrete are all conductive surfaces that you can sit, walk, or stand on to gain the benefits of earthing. Ideally, you can spend 20 to 30 minutes earthing, but even a few minutes can make a big difference.

Earthing is my go-to when I need a mental reset. It's enjoyable, calming, and effective. Feeling grounded is a state of being where we are present, calm, and centered. When we feel grounded, we feel less anxious and more tapped into our power.

# 12
## JUNE

*I honor my beautiful femininity and admire my ability to be at once fluid, nurturing, creative, intuitive, and supportive while fully embracing my power, my purpose, and my path.*

# 13
## JUNE

*I celebrate other people's successes. I avoid comparing myself to anyone else, because we are all on our own individual journey, and there is enough room for everyone to succeed.*

# 14
JUNE

## CONFIDENCE CALENDAR

Confidence and courage go hand in hand. When we're confident, we can act courageously. Grab your journal and planner, because today you're going to schedule daily boosts of confidence.

Start by brainstorming seven things you can do to boost your confidence and write them in your journal. For example, if you enjoy hiking because you love being outdoors and it makes you feel strong, that's one thing. Or perhaps you realize that you haven't celebrated your small successes in a long time. Add that to the list!

After you've written down these seven things, it's time to fill in your confidence calendar. Schedule one for each day of the week. Sunday: Go for a hike! Friday: Take inventory of your small successes this past week, and then take time to celebrate them. Enjoy your week of courageously choosing to focus on the things that boost and nourish your self-confidence.

## 15
### JUNE

*I take calculated risks that propel me forward. I trust in my abilities, my knowledge, and most important, myself! I am in the driver's seat of my life path.*

## 16
### JUNE

"If your fear of being judged is keeping you from implementing ideas that may change your life, what else is that fear holding you back from? Those that take action in spite of fear accomplish great things, while those chained to fear are shouting 'that's impossible.'"

— DEBORAH FRANCIS AND HASHEEM FRANCIS

# 17
## JUNE

*I respect myself, I know my value, and I accept compliments with grace and ease. I love myself and who I am becoming.*

# 18
## JUNE

### NOTE YOUR NONNEGOTIABLES

For today's practice, you're going to make a long list . . . of your nonnegotiables! Nonnegotiables are what we resolutely adhere to; there's no wiggle room and no room for negotiation. Nonnegotiables encompass your standards and boundaries, which is why they should be a top priority in your daily life.

We often think of nonnegotiables in our love life: My partner must be ABC and not do XYZ. These are your relationship nonnegotiables. In your professional life, perhaps a nonnegotiable is not working during the weekend.

For this practice, you can choose to make several columns: one for each area of your life. Or you can make one primary list to revisit and refine over time. Physically writing down your nonnegotiables further solidifies them in your mind and in your reality. When you know exactly what you stand for, you become more resolute and unwavering in your self-confidence.

# 19
## JUNE

---

*I am accountable for my daily interactions, and I take full responsibility for how I treat each person I encounter along the way. Being accountable is empowering, liberating, and rewarding.*

# 20
## JUNE

---

"Courage is like—it's a habitus, a habit, a virtue: You get it by courageous acts. It's like you learn to swim by swimming. You learn courage by couraging."

**—MARY DALY**

# 21

## JUNE

*When self-doubt creeps in, I choose to focus on my strengths and abilities. I am capable of navigating any storm, and I love being the captain of my ship.*

# 22

## JUNE

### SOLSTICE SUN SALUTATIONS

The summer solstice is the longest day of the year. Often in yoga, the solstice is celebrated by doing sun salutations. This simple form of sun salutation can be done with or without a yoga mat. It's an energizing, centering practice you can do anytime.

Stand with your feet hip-distance apart. With an inhale, reach your arms overhead, and with your exhale, bring your hands to heart center. Inhale: arms overhead. Exhale: hands to heart center. You can repeat this simple flow three times or add a few extra steps: Inhale: arms overhead. Exhale: hands to heart as you slowly bow into a forward fold. Inhale for a halfway lift, bringing hands to your shins or thighs. Exhale: forward fold again. With your next inhale, rise all the way to standing, and exhale hands back to heart. That's one round: repeat for three total rounds.

## 23

JUNE

—

*I view obstacles, challenges, and struggles as opportunities for personal growth, so I approach them with curiosity and appreciation. Without challenges, I would remain stagnant.*

## 24

JUNE

—

*I allow myself to feel and process whatever I am going through as a healthy means of release. My connection to my emotions is the gateway to my intuition and self-awareness.*

# 25
## JUNE

---

**TRANSMUTE YOUR WOUNDS**

"Turn your wounds into wisdom" is one of my favorite Oprah Winfrey quotes. It's an important reminder that all our "wounds"—our hurts, disappointments, and/or failures—hold valuable lessons. When we sift through the wound to find the wisdom, then the pain was not in vain.

Often in life, we try to avoid pain or discomfort because we're afraid of it or think we can't handle it. Yet, time after time, in the face of challenges, we prove our doubts wrong! We rise up, make it through, and learn something about ourselves along the way.

Reflect on some of your recent challenges, and then grab your journal and write down a few ways that it worked out better than expected, or showed you your strength, that you are always supported, or what you learned and how it made you stronger. Reflection helps transmute your wounds into your wisdom.

# 26
## JUNE

*The words I speak are the ink that dries on the pages of my experiences, so I choose them carefully. I am the author of my life. Each day is a new chapter.*

# 27
## JUNE

## "Be careful what you say to yourself because you are listening."

**—LISA M. HAYES**

# 28
## JUNE

*Instead of trying to force a certain outcome, I pause and take a step back. When I do this, answers and solutions more easily reveal themselves.*

# 29
JUNE

—

## OASIS DAY OUTLINE

Imagine spending a day in an oasis—an ideal day that feels supportive, balanced, intentional, and, as a result, more fulfilling.

What would your oasis day look like? This can apply to your personal life, professional life, or both. If you think about a typical day in your life, what does it look like? Is it jam-packed, rushed, and hectic? Are there any aspects of your day you want to shift or change? Areas where you're spending too much or not enough time?

The objective is to create a sanctuary wherein your daily responsibilities are approached in a calm, deliberate, and gratifying way. Grab your journal, and outline your oasis day from the moment you wake up to the moment you go to sleep. Then, put it into practice tomorrow.

# 30
JUNE

—

*I have a strong support system of people who love me and want to see me suc-ceed. I ask for support when I need it, and I offer support in return.*

JULY

# 1

## JULY

*I communicate with clarity and confidence. My daily words and actions create my legacy. I do my best, and I am proud of the life I lead. I am a living legend!*

# 2

## JULY

## "The success of every woman should be the inspiration to another. We should raise each other up. Make sure you're very courageous: be strong, be extremely kind, and, above all, be humble."

**—SERENA WILLIAMS**

# 3

## JULY

*My life is a vast portrait of incredible experiences and memories that culminate in the woman I have become, and, for all of this, I am deeply grateful.*

# 4

## JULY

### BAKE IN GRATITUDE

A single thought can influence your entire day! When you first wake up, one positive thought can transform your morning and create a positive ripple effect throughout your day. Taking this one step further, an attitude of gratitude literally shifts your mind's focus.

Here's how it works: The next time you wake up, bake an attitude of gratitude into your day by listing three things you're grateful for before you even get out of bed. Your mind is constantly scanning for thoughts to focus on, and what you focus on expands. When you train your morning brain to focus on gratitude, it will continue finding things to be thankful for throughout the day.

Beginning your morning with a focus on gratitude will make that gratitude reverberate throughout every moment. Wake up and integrate abundance, gratitude, and positivity into your morning. The rest of your day will thank you!

# 5
## JULY

*I am incredibly grateful for my strong, healthy body and everything it does for me. I take care of myself and listen to what my body tells me it needs.*

# 6
## JULY

## "Change the way you look at things and the things you look at change."

**—DR. WAYNE DYER**

# 7
## JULY

*I write my own self-worth narrative. Throughout the day, I consciously choose to speak and think in a way that reflects my value, my abilities, and my intentions.*

# 8

## MIRROR LOVE NOTES

For more than a decade, I've had a practice of leaving myself notes on my bathroom mirror as a visual way to affirm and be reminded of my goals. It's effective!

For your mirror notes, take an honest inventory of where you need a little extra love, support, or motivation. If you're feeling overwhelmed, write yourself a few supportive notes on your mirror (sticky notes or dry-erase markers work great) like "You've got this!" or "Take a deep breath, all is well." Perhaps you want to shower yourself in praise—as you should! Write yourself a few notes as a reminder of how amazing you are: "You are a radiant goddess!" or "I am so proud of you!" or "You are doing a great job!"

Write your mirror love notes today, and, each time you see them, take a moment to really let the message sink in.

# 9
JULY

*My life is not a pass-or-fail experience. I do not subscribe to failure—I either succeed or learn a valuable lesson that will help me reach greater heights next time.*

# 10
### JULY

"Always concentrate on how far you have come, rather than how far you have left to go. The difference in how easy it seems will amaze you."

—HEIDI JOHNSON

# 11
### JULY

*I set realistic goals for myself and follow through with the necessary action needed to accomplish them. Intentional action driven by purpose and passion is my formula for success.*

# 12
## JULY

**MIDDAY MINDFULNESS**

Our days can be busy, which is why a mindful pause can hit the mental reset button and create a moment of calm. Today, take a midday mindfulness break to recalibrate.

Maybe you want to feed two birds with one seed and try this while you eat your lunch. How much awareness can you bring to each bite? How many flavors can you taste? What colors are on your plate? Which ingredients can you smell most strongly? Treat yourself to a fully mindful meal.

Or perhaps you take this practice outside. Fully take in your surroundings, as if for the first time. Wherever you are, what do you see? If there are trees, how many shades of green can you decipher? How does the temperature feel against your skin?

Take a moment to notice any shifts in your mindset or mood. Feel free to revisit this practice often.

## 13
### JULY

---

*Note to self: I love you, I am so incredibly proud of you, and you continue to amaze me every single day. Keep on shining. The world needs your radiance!*

## 14
### JULY

---

"If you know you are on the right track, if you have this inner knowledge, then nobody can turn you off … no matter what they say."

**—BARBARA MCCLINTOCK**

# 15

---

## MIDYEAR CHECK-IN

July marks the middle of the year. This is a great time to take inventory of where you are and where you want to go.

Treat this inventory as your road map for the upcoming year. To start, think about where you want to be one year from today. Then grab your journal and take a few minutes to do a brain dump of the necessary actions or goals you need to set in order to get there.

Next, list the following benchmarks: one month, three months, six months, one year. You can do this in columns, a bubble chart, or whatever makes sense for you visually. Break each benchmark into manageable steps: What actions do you need to take over the next month to get closer to your one-year objective? Over the next three months? List as many steps as needed and commit to taking consistent action to bring your one-year objective into reality.

## 16
### JULY

*Everything in my past has shown me that I am strong enough, intelligent enough, and capable enough to face whatever comes my way. There is always a solution to any problem.*

## 17
### JULY

"Optimism is a happiness magnet. If you stay positive, good things and good people will be drawn to you."

—MARY LOU RETTON

# 18
## JULY

*Today will be a peaceful, positive, and productive day. I am grateful for all the opportunities that are available to me today.*

# 19
## JULY

### TRAIN YOUR BUTTERFLIES

When I walked into the studio to teach my first-ever yoga class, I was so nervous. I told my mentor, who was attending class, that I had butterflies in my stomach. Her reply completely shifted my mindset: "It's not about *not* having butterflies. It's about teaching them to fly in formation."

Public speaking, flying, job interviews, first dates—inevitably, we all encounter nerve-racking experiences that make us feel anxious. What makes you feel nervous? Brainstorm action steps you can take to prepare for it. For example, if it's flying, download a calming meditation, pack a mindfulness coloring book, and create a mantra to repeat to yourself like *I am calm, I am safe, and all is well.*

We can't and shouldn't avoid everything that intimidates us, but we *can* take steps to mitigate the pressure through preparation. Channel that nervous energy and redirect your anxiety into empowered action!

# 20
JULY

---

*I purify my mind with positive, nourishing thoughts that soothe my stress and wring out my worries. I embody my purpose and stay committed to protecting my peace.*

# 21
JULY

---

*My energy attracts the same kind of energy back to me. I expect good things, because I know that when I emit positive energy, I will receive more good in return.*

# 22

## COMPLIMENT CHALLENGE

Giving a sincere compliment is as rewarding as receiving one. When we feel secure and confident enough in ourselves to genuinely admire and compliment others, that's a great feeling! More important, giving compliments also boosts our own self-confidence, so it's a positive feedback loop.

Start by challenging yourself to give one genuine compliment today. Don't overthink it! Whether it's complimenting your colleague on a job well done or telling the woman in front of you in line that she looks beautiful or pulling a family member aside to tell them how proud you are of them, shower someone with a compliment today.

The recipient of your compliment will enjoy the confidence boost and feeling of being acknowledged, and you'll enjoy the sense of selflessly giving someone else praise. The positive feedback loop applies here, too, as they will be more likely to pay someone else a compliment, and thus the giving continues!

## 23
JULY

*I am my own lifelong companion and best friend. I am capable, I am confident, I am in control, and I am exactly where I need to be.*

## 24
JULY

"Don't sit around thinking of all the reasons why you can't do something. Find one good reason why you can do it and focus on that."

**—ZOE RENE**

## 25
JULY

*Every problem has a purpose. Every challenge has a solution. Every person has something to teach me. Every day brings new opportunities.*

# 26
## JULY

### SUPPORT SYSTEM MEDITATION

Having a support system is important for our mental health and overall quality of life. Support systems help us with decision-making and during challenging times. They make us feel seen, heard, valued, respected, and loved, which is empowering! We feel confident and motivated when we feel supported.

Reflect on the supportive people in your life. Perhaps your support system includes your partner, parents, grandparents, siblings, close friends, and/or colleagues. Support can come from other sources, too, like your favorite motivational author or a public figure you admire.

Make a list of these people in your journal, and then find a comfortable seat and close your eyes. One by one, envision each person sitting across from you. Take a moment to send them love and gratitude. Move on to the next person until you've gotten through your list. When you acknowledge the support you have, you recharge your courage and confidence.

# 27
## JULY

*When I recognize all the good in my life, I find peace and contentment.*

# 28
## JULY

---

*I choose to let go of limiting beliefs that are holding me back. I remain open to new ideas, new experiences, and different ways of thinking to find new solutions.*

# 29
## JULY

---

### TWIST IT OUT

There's nothing like a good spinal twist for winding down from your day or any-time you feel a need to release and relax. Twists can increase circulation, release tension in the back muscles, and, as a result, help you feel more relaxed. Spinal twists can help unravel your mental tension and shift your perspective, too.

This is a simple practice you can do sitting in a chair or on the floor, and it only takes a few moments to feel the effects.

From a seated position, sit up tall. Imagine you have a marionette string attached to the crown of your head pulling you skyward. Place your left hand on your right knee and your other hand on your low back. Take a deep inhale, and, with your exhale, gently twist your mid-spine (think upper torso) toward the right. Remain in your twist for three deep breaths, and then switch sides.

## 30
### JULY

*I forgive my past mistakes; they do not define me. I am intelligent. I am an asset. I am a powerhouse! I am wanted, needed, and supported. I belong here!*

## 31
### JULY

*I recognize and honor the light in every living being. I allow my own light to shine brightly as a beacon that reminds others to never dim their radiance.*

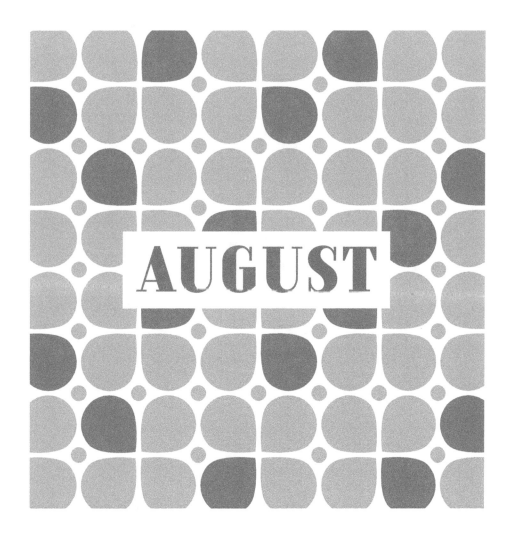

AUGUST

# 1
## AUGUST

---

*I am never too old, and it is never too late. I am content with who I am, where I'm at, and what I have. I will not postpone my joy.*

# 2
## AUGUST

---

*My belief and understanding of all that is possible continues to expand. My success is limitless, and I am grateful for every single opportunity that is speeding my way.*

# 3

---

## ABUNDANCE MINDSET

In *The 7 Habits of Highly Effective People,* Stephen Covey coined the term "abundance mindset," which is the opposite of a lack or scarcity mindset. You cultivate an abundance mindset by doing things that make you feel abundant—whether with your time, your energy, or your thoughts.

You can employ this perspective in many areas of your life, from mindset and physical health to money and mental energy. Examples of a lack-based mindset are feeling unworthy or trapped with no options or being closed-minded. An abundant mindset, in contrast, focuses on personal empowerment, finding new solutions and opportunities, and having the confidence to strike a new path.

Today, create an abundance mindset for yourself. Notice an area in your life where you can shift your thinking. Seek out new opportunities with the belief that they are waiting for you. Choose your thoughts and words wisely and with intention.

# 4

## AUGUST

*Life is truly precious, and every day is priceless, so I greet each morning with gratitude and excitement. I wake up feeling motivated, energized, playful, and inspired.*

# 5

## AUGUST

# "Let us choose for ourselves our path in life, and let us try to strew that path with flowers."

**—ÉMILIE DU CHÂTELET**

# 6

## AUGUST

*My intentions create my reality. I visualize my desire, I believe in my ability to manifest, I take intentional steps to get there, and I allow the process to unfold.*

# 7

## HOW DO YOU LIVE ON PURPOSE?

Have you heard the saying, "May you live every day of your life"? It means that we can be alive but not really *living* our lives to the fullest and instead living on autopilot, simply going through the motions.

So, what does truly *living* every day of your life have to do with living your life *on purpose*? According to author and success coach Katrina Ruth, living on purpose is about "doing what truly matters to you in alignment with your values and beliefs."

Having a purpose produces energy! When we are aligned with our path, doing what we love and finding value and meaning in it, we not only feel fulfilled; we also feel motivated, energized, and ALIVE! We find inspiration in the passionate pursuit of living out our purpose.

Grab your journal, set a timer for 10 minutes, and answer this question: What does living on purpose mean to you?

# 8
AUGUST

*I do not need to apologize for setting healthy boundaries. I do not need to apologize for saying no, not being perfect, or not having time. I respect my needs.*

# 9
AUGUST

"As you get older, you become more comfortable in your skin and comfortable in saying no to things . . . I've also learned that saying no is just as valuable as saying yes. It's something that, I think, comes with age and really having a sense of your self-worth. And then you make choices based on that."

**—MEGHAN MARKLE**

# 10
## AUGUST

---

### DANCE PARTY

Like laughter, music can be the best medicine. Music has the power to change your mood, lift your spirits, and, depending on the type of music, make you feel different emotions—happy, motivated, inspired, energized . . .

Today's mission, if you choose to accept it, is to have a mini dance party for yourself. My favorite place for a dance party is in my living room, but you can do this anywhere you feel most comfortable. Pick out your favorite song (or songs or album—whatever you're in the mood for and have the time for) and turn up the volume!

Move freely and dance like nobody's watching. Dance alone or with someone else—it's your choice. Immerse yourself in the rhythm and get lost in the movement. Dance through any emotions you may be processing, dance to express yourself, or dance to let go—just dance!

# 11
## AUGUST

---

*I have permission to express myself. I am allowed to feel and process any emotions that arise, and trust that these feelings help inform me of my daily needs.*

# 12
## AUGUST

---

*I live my life in awe and with excellence. I pursue my purpose boldly and recognize the potential in everything. I am so incredibly grateful for everything in my life.*

# 13
## AUGUST

---

### WONDERFUL WATERMELON

Did you know that two-thirds of a cup of watermelon is 91 percent water? Watermelon also contains high amounts of vitamin C, as well as lycopene, a powerful antioxidant.

Enter: my go-to watermelon salad recipe that's as simple as it is healthy and as delicious as it is hydrating. Dice or ball your watermelon, toss it in a bowl, and then add anything else you'd like; basil or mint and chopped cucumber or pineapple are all delicious additions. You are the chef, and your taste buds get to decide!

Another fun favorite (and a hit with the kiddos) is watermelon ice cubes. Simply toss your chopped watermelon in a blender, add a bit of lime juice or sweetener (both optional), blend until smooth, and then place in your ice cube tray and freeze until they're ready to enjoy like a bite-sized ice pop .

# 14
## AUGUST

---

"I don't run away from a challenge because I am afraid. Instead, I run toward it because the only way to escape fear is to trample it beneath your feet."

—NADIA COMĂNECI

# 15
## AUGUST

---

*I stay true to my word and honor my commitments. I stand up for myself and my beliefs. I am disciplined and take pride in living my life with integrity.*

# 16
## AUGUST

---

### MAKE YOUR BED

In her book *The Happiness Project*, Gretchen Rubin shares how one of the simplest actions we can take to increase our happiness is to make our beds! Making your bed each morning can lead to improved mood and reduced stress.

Making my bed is part of my morning routine. I love having a nice, neat bed to climb into each night. More important, it nurtures my discipline, productivity, and sense of self-worth and accomplishment.

Making your bed is the first accomplishment of your day! A neat, clean bed helps you feel and be more productive. It takes discipline and thereby establishes a keystone habit—the pillar that sets the tone for the rest of your decisions and actions throughout the day.

Challenge yourself to make your bed every morning this week. Check in with yourself on the seventh morning and notice any shifts you may have experienced.

# 17
AUGUST

"People become really quite remarkable when they start thinking that they can do things. When they believe in themselves they have the first secret of success."

**—NORMAN VINCENT PEALE**

# 18
AUGUST

*I am strong and resilient, and I am doing a great job. I acknowledge how far I've come because I value my progress and each step of my journey.*

# 19
## AUGUST

---

### HABIT HACK

Some habits are ingrained in us since childhood, like brushing our teeth. Others we've cultivated intentionally, like working out or eating healthy. We can also form detrimental habits, like spending too much time on social media or smoking cigarettes.

Habits are formed by repetitive actions consciously enacted until they become easier and eventually maybe even automatic. Knowing this, we can hack our brains and form new self-serving habits.

Think of a positive and realistic habit you'd like to establish, and write it in your journal. Then commit to following through for the next 30 days. Grab your planner and schedule something that supports your new habit every day. Take manageable steps by starting small and building over time.

Remember to stay consistent. Also, be sure to remove any temptations that could break your newly forming habit. As a bonus, check in with yourself weekly to celebrate your milestones.

# 20
## AUGUST

*Everything I encounter is a mirror. Everything I do creates a powerful ripple effect. Every experience provides me with an opportunity to grow, learn, and evolve.*

# 21
## AUGUST

*Like the metamorphosis of a caterpillar into a butterfly, amazing transformation is occurring within me. Free from self-doubt and full of self-confidence, I continue to evolve and spread my wings.*

# 22

### ASTRO DAY!

There's more to knowing and understanding your zodiac signs than reading a weekly horoscope. Astrology can be a fun and insightful tool to gain a new angle of understanding about your likes and dislikes, strengths and personal challenges, personality and relationships, and even your life path and purpose.

There are 12 zodiac signs, each associated with an elemental property (earth, water, air, or fire). We all have a sun, moon, and rising sign, and your specific birth chart is based on planetary alignment at the place and time you were born. Together, these three signs can provide interesting and helpful insights and inform a lot about yourself.

Today, seek out your astrological birth chart! You will need your date and time of birth, plus the city you were born in. From websites to books or having your chart read, there are many resources available to learn about your birth chart.

# 23

AUGUST

*I give myself space and time to learn and progress. I allow myself to be who I am without judgment. I strike my own path and trust in my unique journey.*

# 24
## AUGUST

*I allow myself to be led by my passion and my purpose. I am not pressured by my problems because I know I can always find the solutions I seek.*

# 25
## AUGUST

### FIELD TRIP

Summer is the season to rejoice in the sunny, warm weather and soak up all that Mother Nature has to offer. That's why it's field trip time! You work hard, and you deserve to take time for rest and enjoyment.

This field trip is about going to your happy place, whether it's physically or mentally. Where is your summertime happy place? The beach? A lush meadow? A secluded mountain lake? Maybe it's your childhood home or your favorite park. If you can physically go there, great! Bring sunscreen and your favorite book and enjoy spending time in your happy place.

If you can't physically go to your happy place, then get comfortable, because your field trip is a visualization! Find a quiet space, close your eyes, and slowly observe your happy place in your mind's eye, focusing on as many details as possible. (This visualization practice can also help you fall asleep!)

# 26
## AUGUST

---

*I am who I surround myself with. I only invite people aboard my ship who I know will help me navigate the waters, not drag me down into the depths.*

# 27
## AUGUST

---

*I love me for me. The more I love all parts of me, the more I accept myself as I am. I release the need to seek approval from others.*

# 28
## AUGUST
---

### SENSORY STROLL

A sensory stroll brings mindful presence to the simple act of walking. It is straight-forward and can be done anywhere—at home or even in a shopping mall. But don't let the simplicity fool you. Mindful walking is an effective and enjoyable way to help relieve stress, reduce anxiety, and increase concentration.

Doing this barefoot outside is ideal, but it isn't necessary. The only necessity is that you can take at least 10 or 15 steps in one direction (or in a circle). Decide your walking route, set a timer for 5 to 10 minutes, and begin.

Focus on your breathing. Take deep, full breaths as you walk slowly. Keep your gaze a few steps in front of your feet, bring your awareness to each foot as it lifts off the ground, and feel the surface beneath you. What else can you notice? Focus on making this a meditative sensory experience.

# 29
## AUGUST
---

*I gather within me all the determination and dedication I can muster, and I continue to amaze myself with my daily advancement. Each calculated action creates a lasting impact.*

# 30
## AUGUST

---

"I believe that fortitude is key. More than anything, be consistent. Go at it. Go at it. Go at it. When you succeed, don't forget the responsibility of making somebody else succeed with you."

**—ANTONIA NOVELLO**

# 31
## AUGUST

---

*I make a conscious decision to seek and embody peace despite any inevitable challenges that arise because* whether I resist or persist, the choice is fully mine.

SEPTEMBER

# 1

SEPTEMBER

—

*When I immerse myself in my purpose, I feel confident and driven, capable and calm, passionate and inspired, and courageous and powerful.*

# 2

SEPTEMBER

—

## REVEL REFLECTION

Today, stand in front of the mirror and tap into your awareness. Feel the floor and the earth beneath you, rising up to support you, reminding you that you are always supported. Embrace the sensation of feeling grounded.

Thank your legs for all the incredible places and distances they've carried you. Feel their strength. Move up to your stomach and core—your place of personal power—then over your heart space where your ability to love and be loved resides. Take an extra moment here to feel that love for yourself. Bask in that love. Now bring your gaze to your own eyes and stare deeply into them, inviting that love to wash over you like a warm hug. As you continue to gaze into the mirror at your own reflection, celebrate and revel in your own incredible beingness.

# 3
## SEPTEMBER

—

*I trust myself. I am confident in the decisions I make and the actions I take. Today is a great day to be proud of myself and how far I have come!*

# 4
## SEPTEMBER

—

"It is so liberating to really know what I want, what truly makes me happy, what I will not tolerate. I have learned that it is no one else's job to take care of me but me."

—BEYONCÉ

# 5

SEPTEMBER

—

*When I am confident, there is no competition. I do not shrink myself to be accepted by others. There is enough room for everyone to blossom and flourish.*

# 6

SEPTEMBER

—

## MORNING MEDITATION

Often what keeps people from starting a meditation practice is the misconception that it is challenging or off-limits if you're not "spiritual enough." But know that making the effort and doing what you can on your terms *is* enough.

Find a form of meditation that works for you, whether it's a guided meditation app, playing soft ambient music and sitting in stillness for a few minutes, or setting a timer for three minutes to simply sit and breathe.

Perhaps you add a mantra like "I am grounded" or "I am at peace" to focus on and repeat to yourself. Try it! With your inhale, say, "I am grounded," and on your exhale, say, "I am peaceful." Or you can break it up: Inhale and say, "I am" and with your exhale, say, "grounded."

Meditate your own way and give yourself the true gift of a mindful morning.

# 7
## SEPTEMBER

*I am not in a rush, and I do not need to do it all now. I can calmly do one thing at a time, and that is good enough!*

# 8
## SEPTEMBER

## "Almost everything will work again if you unplug it for a few minutes, including you."

**—ANNE LAMOTT**

# 9
## SEPTEMBER

*I am worthy of the praise and compliments I receive. There is no need to change any aspect of myself—I am loved and accepted exactly as I am.*

# 10
## SEPTEMBER

---

### CREATE YOUR NOT-TO-DO LIST

Just as there are plenty of things we should do for our overall well-being, there are also plenty of things that we're better off *not* doing. For today's practice, create the inverse of a typical to-do list: a no-list, or a not-to-do list.

What is something that would be self-serving for you to *not* do anymore? For example, if you are a people pleaser and have a hard time saying no to things you honestly don't want to do, then add "Saying yes when I don't want to" to your not-to-do list. This helps you create and maintain healthy boundaries.

Grab your journal and list five not-to-do items. The point of this practice is to identify certain things, choices, or behaviors that don't align with your authentic needs, and then use this list often to help eliminate them and empower yourself in the process.

# 11
## SEPTEMBER

---

*If I do not try, there is no chance for success. If I do try, regardless of the outcome, I emerge victorious in my lessons, gains, and forward progression.*

# 12

SEPTEMBER

---

"I always go back to my grandmother's advice to me . . . the first time I fell and hurt myself. She said to me, 'Honey, at least falling on your face is a forward movement.'"

**—PAT MITCHELL**

# 13

SEPTEMBER

---

*I forgive myself for past mistakes, I treat myself with love in the present, and I envision the future I seek, always striving to do my best and let the rest go.*

# 14

---

### FIVE-MINUTE RESET

Rest, self-care, and doing things that fill you up is important, but inevitably there will be days when you simply don't have a lot of time. Yet it's in these times of being particularly busy that you most need a moment to hit the reset button.

For today's practice, try a few things that don't require a lot of time but do provide a nice reset for your physical and mental state of being. Add one or a few of the following activities into your day for a quick and effective reset:

- Drink a full glass of water slowly.
- Give yourself or someone else a genuine compliment.
- Stretch or move your body.
- Take five deep breaths, smile, and then take five more deep breaths.
- Read or write a paragraph.
- Send a friend a kind message.
- Name three things you're grateful for.
- Take a walk around the block.

# 15
## SEPTEMBER
---

*It is okay to not be okay. It's okay to take a break, to not know the answer, to say no, make mistakes, change my mind, or ask for help.*

# 16
## SEPTEMBER
---

*Rest is my soul's elixir. The most productive thing I can do is rest when I feel tired or drained. The time I take to pause brings me comfort and clarity.*

# 17

## SELF-ASSESSMENT AFFIRMATION

Executive coach Bonnie Marcus combines self-assessment with positive affirmations for her clients. It's an effective way to customize an affirmation for yourself based on your current needs.

Start with your self-assessment. If, for example, you currently struggle with finding motivation, think about what you would have or feel like if you *were* feeling motivated and then create a statement that supports this current challenge: "If I were more motivated, I would accomplish the goals I set for myself this year." The final step is to create a positive affirmation to help solve the need that your self-assessment identified: "I have an endless supply of motivation, and I know I can accomplish my goals!"

We often get swept up in the emotions of a challenge before being able to assess and find the necessary solution. Engaging in self-assessment helps pinpoint your current challenges and find a constructive way to move forward.

# 18
## SEPTEMBER

---

*I choose to consciously respond to challenges rather than automatically react to them. I embrace challenges for the lessons they impart.*

# 19
## SEPTEMBER

---

"We may encounter many defeats, but we must not be defeated. It may even be necessary to encounter the defeat so that we can know who we are. So that we can see, oh, that happened, and I rose. I did get knocked down flat in front of the whole world, and I rose. I didn't run away; I rose right where I'd been knocked down."

**—MAYA ANGELOU**

# 20

## SEPTEMBER

---

*My lowest lows help me reach my greatest heights. My most challenging days help me grow. Without rain, spring flowers wouldn't bloom. Without hardship, my happiness wouldn't be as meaningful.*

# 21

## SEPTEMBER

---

### FOLLOW YOUR BLISS

When you think of bliss, what feelings does it evoke? When we do what we love, our sense of satisfaction, fulfillment, and passion for life grows.

Today's practice is reflection: What brings you bliss? How can you insert more bliss into your daily life? If you love music, for example, why not create a playlist of your favorite songs to accompany you throughout your day? In life, it truly is the small things that add color and vibrancy to our experiences, and when we embrace what we love as part of our day, we're following our bliss.

When we make a practice of doing what we love and enjoy on a regular basis, we nourish ourselves from the inside out so we can, in turn, give our very best to our loved ones, our community, career, goals, and daily interactions.

# 22

---

*Everything I desire is available to me. As a conscious creator, I transform my desires into reality by always remaining aware of the power and potential that exists within me.*

# 23

---

"The thing that has surprised me the most about launching a company is that when you move through fear and resistance, new strength and resilience that you never knew you had, takes control."

**—LALAH DELIA**

# 24
## SEPTEMBER

_I am a magnet for success. Opportunities come to me often and with ease. I am always supported and have the resources needed to succeed. I am thriving!_

# 25
## SEPTEMBER

### DRESS FOR SUCCESS

Dressing for success can boost your self-confidence. When we dress in a way that makes us feel confident, we embody that confidence, and it shows! And when we feel confident, we feel good about ourselves.

While this concept may feel surface level, there is merit to it. When we feel confident in what we wear, we are more inclined to think critically, feel more empowered, convey success, and garner respect.

With this in mind, the next time you leave your house, whether it is to go to work or to the grocery store, dress in a way that makes you feel good. Pick out one of your favorite outfits, add your favorite accessory, and rock it! Whatever style or look makes you feel your best—wear it loud, proud, and unapologetically.

## 26
### SEPTEMBER

*I protect my inner peace and nourish myself by setting boundaries. I do not need to justify my needs to anyone. I commit to my boundaries to honor my self-worth.*

## 27
### SEPTEMBER

*Everyone, including me, is doing their best, and no one is perfect. When we greet each other with compassion, empathy, and understanding, we all benefit and flourish.*

# 28

SEPTEMBER

---

## ACCOUNTABILITY PARTNERS

Accountability is a key ingredient in staying motivated. Having someone to hold you accountable can be a huge help in reaching your goals.

For this practice, think of someone you'd like to have as your accountability partner and ask them if they are willing. You can then set a time to have a quick coffee, phone call, or chat to check in and share your weekly goals and intentions. Set a day to check in each week (or biweekly or monthly) and then stick to it.

Make it something to look forward to, whether it is a happy hour video call each week or a monthly check-in you do with intention. Even if it's just a quick weekly text message or email to share your goals and intentions, knowing you have someone to cheer you on, show support, and help hold you accountable can do so much for your motivation and dedication.

# 29

SEPTEMBER

———

*I am the reason others feel seen, heard, honored, and supported. I am this support system for others, just as I allow others to be this support system for me.*

# 30

SEPTEMBER

———

*I am deeply grateful for my body, my mind, my health, and my unique abilities. Today and every day, I celebrate and embrace all the amazing qualities make me who I am*

OCTOBER

# 1

OCTOBER

*I encounter blessings, beauty, and bounty on a daily basis. I accept all these gifts with open arms and a grateful heart. Life is good, and I embrace each moment.*

# 2

OCTOBER

## "You are not stuck. Everything, everything, everything is temporary."

**—CHANI NICHOLAS**

# 3

OCTOBER

*I am compassionate and kind to others and myself. I surround myself with people who love and care about me and who uplift and nourish my soul.*

# 4

---

## CELEBRATE THE SMALL STUFF

Cue Kool & The Gang's song "Celebration," because today is all about celebrating your small successes!

When I was a new entrepreneur experiencing total burnout, one of the biggest lessons I learned (aside from taking breaks and time to rest) is to celebrate the small successes along the way. When we do this, we acknowledge our progress, which is immensely motivating. We also give ourselves credit for what we've accomplished, which fortifies our confidence and fuels us to keep going.

Reflect on a few of your recent accomplishments and victories. It could be as simple as finally getting caught up on email, finishing a big project, or receiving a nice compliment from your boss. Choose something you want to acknowledge and celebrate, and then take time to do precisely that! Do something nice for yourself, and soak up the wonderful sense of satisfaction and accomplishment that comes with it.

# 5
## OCTOBER

*I am generous with what I have to give. What I offer freely, I receive back tenfold.
I am in a constant state of giving and receiving, and my cup overflows.*

# 6
## OCTOBER

## "You're braver than you believe, and stronger than you seem, and smarter than you think."

**—A. A. MILNE**

# 7
## OCTOBER

*I choose what I do with my time and when. The "right time" and "perfect timing"
may never come, so I follow my own clock and embrace opportunities as
they arise.*

# 8

## MAP YOUR WEEK

Grab your planner or calendar and list your top five priority to-dos for the week. Next, list any additional to-dos and any other weekly responsibilities, like checking email. Now you're ready to schedule everything into your workweek. Assign one of your priority to-dos for each day of the week. Then disperse the remaining weekly responsibilities as evenly as possible.

Keep it realistic—do not overload your days. You may find it helpful to select certain days for certain tasks. If you find yourself spending too much time on email, and if you are able, schedule in 30 minutes each day to take a break. As Oprah Winfrey says, "Discipline comes from doing." Establishing discipline in your workweek will help you feel productive in a routine that keeps you motivated and inspired.

# 9

OCTOBER

*I am resourceful, innovative, and creative. I am endlessly inspired by my inner world as well as the outer world, and I draw from them like a bottomless well.*

# 10

"Courage is the price that life exacts for
granting peace."

**—AMELIA EARHART**

# 11

OCTOBER

*My past proves that when I keep showing up and put in the work, I am rewarded.
I am capable of achieving my goals, and I enjoy the steps along the way!*

# 12

---

## THE SAID PRINCIPLE

The SAID principle, which stands for specific adaptation to imposed demands, states that what you train, you improve. Rooted in sports science, this principle means that the body will adapt under stress and continue to improve in whatever forms of stress you place on it. For example, if you are learning how to play the piano, the longer you practice, the better you'll become. With time and repetition, your motor skills will improve, and the part of your brain responsible for all the finger movements will actually grow!

Applying the SAID principle to your self-confidence, the more often you take small steps and regular actions toward building your confidence, the more confidence you'll have as a result. What is a small step you can take today to boost your self-confidence? What are some regular actions to help you get there? Commit to these daily and watch the SAID principle take effect.

# 13

OCTOBER

---

*I choose to view my life as the incredible gift that it is. My life is vibrant and ever-evolving, and I have so much to be grateful for.*

# 14
## OCTOBER

---

*I love getting to know who I am. When I shine an introspective light on myself, I see an incredible woman who I am getting to know better each day!*

# 15
## OCTOBER

---

### MANIFESTATION MAGNET

If you emit negativity, you'll be met with more negativity. If you emit positivity, you'll encounter more positivity. If you always expect bad things to happen, you create a stronger likelihood of them happening. The same applies for good things.

Let's say you want to find a supportive, inspiring friend. In your journal, map out one step you can take each day to make this a reality. Day one, list the attributes you want this new friend to have. Day two, imagine how you'd feel when you spend time together. Day three, start to envision the ways this friendship would inspire you. Take a small step each day until it becomes a reality. It may take a week or a year, but trust that it will happen.

This approach is part mental (focusing on what you want to attract and believing it will happen), and part action (the steps you take to get there).

## 16
### OCTOBER

—

*I am a manifestation magnet, attracting the life I want to lead through the words I speak and the actions I take. I actively attract that which I seek.*

## 17
### OCTOBER

—

# "Being brave is not being unafraid but feeling the fear and doing it anyway."

**—GLORIA STEINEM**

## 18
### OCTOBER

—

*I am self-confident, and I deserve to feel good about everything that I do and everything I am. I possess the tools, support, and knowledge to be successful and content.*

# 19
## OCTOBER

### DO A MOCK INTERVIEW

When I was a teenager, my dad and I would practice mock interviews. With his background as a high school vocational teacher, my dad knew the value of practice and repetition, as well as the confidence-building that came with it. Through the simple act of practicing interview questions, I built up the valuable skill of having confidence under pressure, which has served me well in life.

This practice can apply to different scenarios as well, like social interactions or conflict resolution. If you have someone you can do this with, great! Have them ask you a series of questions that will challenge your poise under pressure.

You can also practice this alone in front of a mirror. There's a lot of power in practicing in the mirror—it helps you fine-tune your presentation, which, in turn, builds major confidence! Put this to the test and experience the results for yourself.

# 20
## OCTOBER

*I take every opportunity to shower myself in praise, love, and acceptance. This is how I take responsibility for my self-confidence and self-worth.*

# 21

OCTOBER

"As you become more clear about who you really are, you'll be better able to decide what is best for you—the first time around."

**—OPRAH WINFREY**

# 22

OCTOBER

*When I wake up each morning, I greet the day ahead, knowing that the world is my oyster. With gratitude, I enjoy each day for the precious pearl it is.*

# 23

___

## PLAN YOUR PERFECT MORNING ROUTINE

Routines help us stay disciplined and productive. A morning routine can be as simple as drinking a glass of water, exercising, and eating breakfast before work. Alternatively, a routine can be detailed, structured, or in-depth. Set yours up today!

Pro tip: Start by hydrating. Slowly sip a glass of room-temperature lemon water. Then engage in several activities you'd like to incorporate into your morning routine. If you are an avid reader, set aside 15 minutes to read. If you want more energy and focus, add a 5-minute meditation and/or 30-minute exercise.

A mindful morning is one that is experienced slowly and intentionally. Regardless of how you create your routine, know that by doing a few things that bring you joy or support your wellness, you set yourself up for a successful day!

# 24

## OCTOBER

---

*I am disciplined, determined, resourceful, and resilient. I channel these qualities to show up as my best, most confident self every day and in all that I do.*

# 25

## OCTOBER

---

*I always look for the good in every situation. Challenging times are there to teach me and help me progress. Thanks to the defeats, I can appreciate the triumphs.*

# 26
## OCTOBER

---

**SHAKE IT UP**

Amid life's ebbs and flows, we encounter times of feeling motivated, just as we encounter times of feeling stagnant. The best thing to do when you're feeling unmotivated, uninspired, or downright stuck? Shake things up!

Where do you want or need to shake things up a bit? If it's in your home, take some time to rearrange your furniture, wear something from the back of your closet, or spruce up your favorite room. If it's more of a stagnation in your routine, try taking a different route home, swap out your morning coffee for tea, or add a new self-care practice into your evening. If you're feeling unorganized, take this opportunity to tidy up, reduce clutter, or finally tackle that junk drawer or closet that's been on your list.

Shaking things up hits the reset button on your mindset and helps you feel motivated, energized, and in control.

# 27
## OCTOBER

---

*I am my own hero. I am the bridge over the bumps in the road. Like a lit match in a pitch-black room, my light can illuminate any darkness.*

# 28
## OCTOBER

"In order to make anything a reality, you have to dream about it first. In many ways, our audacity to imagine helps push the boundaries of possibility."

**—ADORA SVITAK**

# 29
## OCTOBER

*Whether it is a fear of failure, rejection, or inadequacy, everything I want is waiting on the other side of my fears, rooting me on.*

# 30

---

## TREAT YOURSELF

Today's practice is no tricks, all treats—treating *yourself,* that is! It's important to solidify simple self-care practices that help you stay calm, cool, and collected. If you already have a few favorite self-care practices or want to create your own, great! Schedule in some time to treat yourself to your favorite one today. If not, or if you're looking for fresh inspiration, you can choose one (or a few) from this list:

- Schedule a nap into your day (or go to bed early).
- Get out in nature.
- Spend time meditating.
- Take a warm Epsom salt bath (essential oils are a pleasant addition).
- Snuggle up with a good book and a soothing cup of tea.
- Cook your favorite healthy meal and enjoy a candlelight dinner at home.

Self-care is an investment in yourself and crucial for maintaining your overall wellness.

# 31

OCTOBER

---

*Fear is False Evidence Appearing Real. It does not make me Forget Everything And Run. I move past my fear by facing it head-on.*

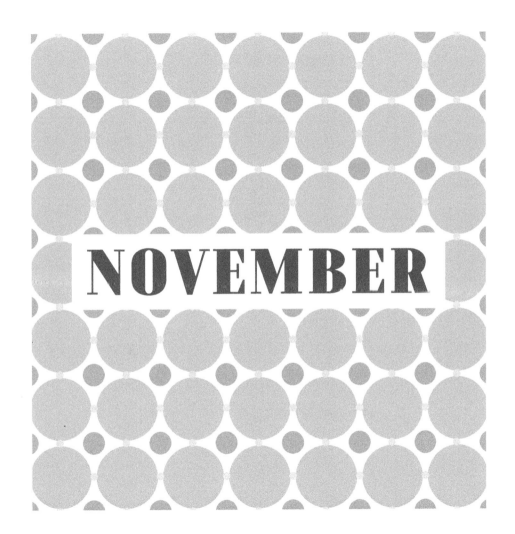

NOVEMBER

# 1

## NOVEMBER

*My life is a rich culmination of abundance, beauty, growth, and connection. I have so much to be grateful for. And so I say, "Thank you, thank you, thank you."*

# 2

## NOVEMBER

## "We do not have to become heroes overnight. Just a step at a time, meeting each thing that comes up, seeing it as not as dreadful as it appears, discovering that we have the strength to stare it down."

**—ELEANOR ROOSEVELT**

# 3

NOVEMBER

*Everything in my life is a vehicle for transformation. Everything I experience is a container that holds my collective experiences that form my identity.*

# 4

NOVEMBER

## BODY SCAN

Performing a body scan is a simple way to create a sense of calm for both mind and body. This is ideal to do in bed at night before you go to sleep but can be done any time of day. All you need is a quiet place and an area where you can relax.

When you're ready, lie down, get comfortable, and, with your eyes open or closed, begin to breathe deeply in and out through your nose. Allow your entire body to soften and relax.

As you continue to breathe deeply, slowly scan your body from the crown of your head to the tips of your toes. Where are you holding any tension? Where can you soften and sink deeper into the surface beneath you? Unfurrow your brows, relax your jaw, and unclench your muscles. Use each breath to help your body rest and be held in the stillness.

# 5
## NOVEMBER

*Nonattachment to expectations helps me find a deeper state of peace and contentment. When I recognize the beauty and abundance all around me, my life becomes lighter and brighter.*

# 6
## NOVEMBER

## "For it's our grief that gives us our gratitude, Shows us how to find hope, if we ever lose it."

**—AMANDA GORMAN**

# 7
## NOVEMBER

*I trust my wisdom and inner knowingness. From this place, I stand confidently in my decisions and own my ability to navigate life with grace and ease.*

# 8

---

## BREATHE

Acronyms are helpful ways to remember your intentions. The acronym BREATHE works twofold: It stands for a powerful series of steps to help you slow down and also reminds you to breathe, which is one of the best and quickest ways to slow down and recenter.

BREATHE stands for:

- **B**e kind to yourself.
- **R**emember things you're grateful for.
- **E**ase your body.
- **A**llow yourself to slow down.
- **T**ake a moment to relax.
- **H**ealth is your priority.
- **E**ase your mind.

For example, pause to focus on gratitude to shift your mindset and be present. Tune in to what your body needs. Does it want to move or be cared for in some way? Give yourself permission to relax. Practice a technique for slowing your racing thoughts to ease your mind.

# 9

*Like a river flowing downstream, my life is a beautiful journey, and I embrace every twist and turn for the adventure it is and the beauty it holds.*

# 10

"I want to be brave with my life...We can choose courage or we can choose comfort, but we can't have both. Not at the same time."

—BRENÉ BROWN

# 11

NOVEMBER

---

*I do not let my fears, doubts, or hesitations define me or dictate my decisions.*

# 12

NOVEMBER

---

## WHAT'S YOUR ENNEAGRAM TYPE?

Personality tests are commonly used as helpful tools in our personal and professional lives. From romantic relationships to choosing the best career path, personality tests can reveal a lot about ourselves and the people in our lives.

Enter the Enneagram personality system. This unique personal assessment approach is often referred to as the "GPS of wisdom" and can be a useful tool for bringing more compassion to the way we view ourselves and others. Knowing your Enneagram type better helps you understand your behaviors; knowing others' types will help you understand theirs.

There are nine Enneagram types: Perfectionist, Helper, Achiever, Individualist, Investigator, Skeptic, Enthusiast, Leader, and Peacemaker. Today, do some online research to find out yours by reading the descriptions of the nine types to see which one you most identify with. Many online resources on this topic also include an Enneagram test, or you can find a professional to facilitate.

# 13

NOVEMBER

—

*I live in alignment with the vision I hold for my life. I approach each day with a thankful heart and adventurous spirit. Today will be an amazing day!*

# 14

NOVEMBER

—

*I proudly live from a place of integrity. My actions lead by example and create a positive ripple effect. I am an inspiring role model for other women.*

# 15

---

## SELF-TALK OVERHAUL

Have you heard about the experiment where a plant with the word "love" next to it grows and thrives, while a plant with the word "hate" next to it withers and dies? This example illustrates the power of words.

With this in mind, pay attention to your self-talk today. Become aware of certain words or phrases you use that may not be in your best interest. Here are a few common examples: "I'm too busy," "I can't," or "I hope." These phrases are defeating and limiting. Compare the following statements: "I hope I can land that job!" versus "I can land that job, and I will."

It's not so much about permanently eliminating certain words from your vocabulary; it's about reshaping and also consciously choosing to use them in the right context for personal empowerment. Choose your words with intention and self-awareness. The words you speak actively shape your perception of reality.

# 16

### NOVEMBER

—

*I release any self-doubt. I strengthen my positive self-talk muscle and remove myself from destructive tendencies.*

# 17

### NOVEMBER

—

## WRITE YOURSELF A LETTER OF RECOMMENDATION

It can be hard to give ourselves praise or even recognize our own gifts. Many people struggle with speaking highly of themselves or have been told it's conceited to do so. Yet one of the most powerful affirmations we can do for ourselves is to sing our own praises, acknowledge all that makes us unique and wonderful, and actually soak up that praise like you would the last bit of soup with a piece of bread.

If you asked your peer, colleague, or mentor to write a letter of recommendation for you, how would they describe you? How would your best friend, mother, or grandmother describe you?

Grab your journal, and write this letter of recommendation for yourself as if you were one of your colleagues, peers, or loved ones. Be sure to sing all your praises, list all your strengths, and take a full page to do so.

# 18
## NOVEMBER

—

*Challenging times remind me of my strength, ground me in my purpose, and bring out the very best in me because I rise to the occasion and emerge better for it.*

# 19
## NOVEMBER

—

## "I'd rather regret the risk that didn't work out than the chances I didn't take at all."

**—SIMONE BILES**

# 20

---

## DIY ELECTROLYTE WATER

Electrolytes are an important part of hydration and fortify crucial functions in the body, including neurological, cardiovascular, cellular, and muscle function. Sea salt contains sodium, potassium, and magnesium. When dissolved in water, sea salt converts into ions, which the body needs to function optimally.

You might be thinking, *You want me to drink salt for hydration?* While it may sound counterintuitive, sea salt helps you stay hydrated—the trace minerals increase the electrolytes in your body. So, go ahead and pour yourself a glass of filtered water. Stir in a pinch of sea salt. (I use Himalayan salt.) You can also add a squeeze of lemon, which has an alkaline effect on your body and contains electrolytes, too.

This DIY electrolyte water rehydrates your body, tastes great, and helps you recover after exercise. It's a simple way to support healthy brain and heart function and boost your overall wellness. Cheers!

# 21
## NOVEMBER

---

*My time is a precious commodity so I choose to always make the best of it. When I value and honor my time, I inspire others to do the same.*

# 22
## NOVEMBER

---

"You've got to say no to the things that don't honor you, NO to the things that don't bring you joy, NO to the things that don't bring you peace, and you don't have to explain your no!!"

—IYANLA VANZANT

# 23

## NOVEMBER

—

*I stand firmly in my boundaries and put my needs first. I protect my time, my values, and my priorities because my self-love dictates my self-worth.*

# 24

## NOVEMBER

—

### PAY IT FORWARD

I'll never forget the first time I witnessed the powerful act of someone paying it forward. I was a young waitress, and a gentleman approached me with his credit card, stating he'd like to treat one of my tables. He didn't know them and didn't want any recognition. He simply said that someone in front of him in line had paid for his coffee the day before, which inspired him to pay it forward by buying someone else's meal.

There are many forms of paying it forward. Perhaps you find yourself at a coffee shop today and surprise the person behind you in line by buying their coffee. You can also pay it forward with your time by taking a Saturday to do volunteer work or helping an elderly person with their groceries.

Look for opportunities to pay it forward today and enjoy the satisfaction of performing a selfless act.

# 25

NOVEMBER

―

*I see every day for the precious and fleeting gift it is, which allows me to remain present and grateful. Each day when I wake up, I say thank you.*

# 26

NOVEMBER

―

*I am so incredibly thankful for all that I have and all that I am. I pause to reflect on all that I have to be grateful for often.*

# 27

## GRATITUDE JOURNAL

Eckhart Tolle says, "Acknowledging all the good that you already have in your life is the foundation for all abundance." Gratitude journaling is the practice of taking a moment to acknowledge all the good that's in your life. This can be as simple as writing down three to five things, big or small, that you're grateful for. You can also write about certain things that easily bring you gratitude.

Grab your journal and choose from these prompts or create your own:

- Write a paragraph about your favorite pet, past or present.
- Write a paragraph about your closest loved one and what you most admire about them.
- What are you best at? Write and reflect on your top three talents.
- What are you most looking forward to this year?
- What's one person, place, or thing that makes you happy? Why?

Focusing on gratitude is a simple way to boost your mood and your mindset.

# 28
## NOVEMBER

*I choose to be compassionate and forgiving for my own benefit. This benefits me, my health, and my peace of mind as much as it benefits others.*

# 29
## NOVEMBER

## "It's important to be unique, even if it makes others uncomfortable."

**—JANELLE MONÁE**

# 30
## NOVEMBER

*I partner with peace, I hold on to my happiness, and I remain grounded in gratitude. I choose to live my life with joy—and what a wonderful life it is!*

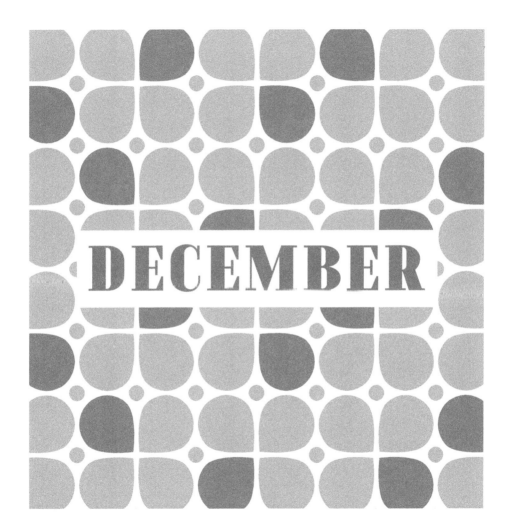

DECEMBER

# 1

## DECEMBER

*I commit to investing in my self-care as a statement of my value and worth. Through this practice, I establish healthy boundaries and nourish my heart, mind, and soul.*

# 2

## DECEMBER

"The mind is so powerful. What we believe is what we manifest in our lives. So believe that you are valuable and worthy and strong and loved and joyful and brave and unique and powerful beyond measure."

**—FAITH BROUSSARD CADE**

# 3

## DECEMBER

---

*I am in control of my day and how I respond to anything that happens.*

# 4

## DECEMBER

---

### BREATH AWARENESS

Pause a moment and take a deep breath. As you exhale, allow your shoulders and jaw to relax. As you inhale, feel the oxygen flowing through your body. Repeat four more rounds—deep and full inhales and exhales in and out through your nose.

Now, begin to rub each fingertip against your thumb, one finger per inhale and exhale. If you feel comfortable, allow your eyes to close and focus on the sensation of linking your breath to the motion.

Next, bring your awareness to your torso. As you inhale, feel the oxygen expand in your stomach, then ribs, and all the way up to your chest and collarbone. As you exhale, feel the oxygen leaving your body until you gently press out the last of your previous breath, before repeating.

Stay in this breath awareness practice for five minutes, exploring the sensations of your deep, conscious breathing.

# 5
## DECEMBER

*I am introspective and self-aware. I love exploring my inner thoughts and getting to know myself on a deeper level so I can better support my needs.*

# 6
## DECEMBER

## "No is a necessary magic. No draws a circle around you with chalk and says, 'I have given enough.'"

**—MCKAYLA ROBBIN**

# 7
## DECEMBER

*I make the conscious choice to envision and expect the best. I deserve good things and know that when I visualize the outcome I want, I attract it.*

# 8

## ABUNDANCE THEORY REALIZED

Have you ever reached into your jacket pocket and found money from the last time you wore it? Or found a dollar on the ground? It's a pleasant surprise that makes you feel abundant, right?

Plant money for yourself today to find later so you can experience a tactile feeling of abundance. Pick something you won't wear until the spring and put money in the pocket—it can be one dollar or any amount you'd like—then put it away in your closet until the time comes to wear it again.

Abundance theory postulates that nurturing a sense of personal abundance will make you feel more abundant, and, as a result, attract more abundance to you. Abundance is the feeling of plenitude regardless of your literal finances. So, when you later find the money, you'll feel bountiful while being reminded of all the abundance in your life.

# 9

*I remain anchored in authenticity. I speak my truth and stand up for myself and what's right. When I stand strong in my beliefs, I find my power and my voice.*

# 10
## DECEMBER

"Putting yourself out there is hard, but it's so worth it. I don't think anyone who has ever spoken out, or stood up or had a brave moment, has regretted it. It's empowering and confidence-building and inspiring. Not only to other people, but to yourself."

—MEGAN RAPINOE

# 11
## DECEMBER

*My life improves and my awareness expands in direct proportion to my ability to recognize all the good, all the growth, and everything that happens as a result of my efforts.*

# 12

## QUICK Q&A FOR CONFIDENCE

Grab your journal and respond to this series of questions to help you pinpoint any areas of your life where you can enhance your sense of self-confidence and motivation:

- List one simple way you can feel more organized and in control this week.
- List three things you are passionate about that bring you joy. What can you do this week to fuel these passions?
- Reflect on a recent experience that made you feel confident and motivated. Why did it make you feel this way?
- Are there any areas of your life where you struggle with self-acceptance and self-confidence? What actions can you take to overcome this?
- List five people in your life who inspire and motivate you. Next to each name, list a few ways they inspire you.
- Is there anything standing between you and feeling motivated? What action steps can you take to move past this?

# 13
## DECEMBER
—

*I embrace the incredible gift of being alive. I refuse to take anything for granted and acknowledge the sacredness of all existence. I take time to sit with my gratitude often.*

# 14
## DECEMBER
—

*Like a shadow cast in the sunlight, my gratitude surrounds me and walks with me everywhere I go. I emanate gratitude, and, in turn, I attract more abundance.*

# 15

---

## MENTAL WELLNESS BREAK

It's simple but undeniable: When we don't take time to rest, we won't have anything left to give. While this is important during the holiday season, it's true all year long.

For your wellness break, take a full day or spread out the following suggestions over several days. The point is to dedicate this time to and for yourself.

- **Step away from your devices!** If you're able to shut off your phone and avoid checking email, do it! Opt for reading over watching TV. When you feel the urge to check notifications, take three deep breaths instead.
- **Do something you love.** Have you been wanting to try a new recipe? Are you and a dear friend overdue for a get-together? Has your favorite hobby been waiting for you on the back burner?

Indulge in your mental wellness break, and emerge feeling refreshed, renewed, and inspired.

# 16
## DECEMBER

—

*I approach life one step at a time. I begin, and then I continue what I started. I believe in my own abilities—there's no need for outside validation.*

# 17
## DECEMBER

—

*I trust my ability to bring my dreams into reality. I do my best every day as my commitment to myself. I put in the work consistently. I believe in my vision.*

# 18

## DECEMBER

---

### WRITE A LETTER YOU WON'T SEND

When you're upset with someone, writing is a healthy outlet to speak your mind and vent so you can let the anger go and stop spending energy on it. The idea here is to *not* send the letter. You may even tear it up and throw it away.

Whether it's past or present, someone you see every day or haven't talked to in years, it can be a helpful, productive release to get your feelings out and onto the page. This process also works on yourself. If you've been harboring any negative feelings toward yourself, now is the time to address them.

This might be a letter of forgiveness or a letter addressing how you're ready to let go of whatever it is you're holding on to (or that's holding you back). Today, take time to get it out and trust that this practice will help you process these emotions and move on.

# 19

## DECEMBER

---

*I am grateful for every single person in my life. Everyone is here to teach me something about myself, just as I am here to learn from and teach others.*

# 20

"We need to accept that we don't always make the right decisions, that we'll screw up royally sometimes—understanding that failure is not the opposite of success, it's part of success."

**—ARIANNA HUFFINGTON**

# 21

---

## WINTER SOLSTICE SALUTATIONS

The winter solstice is the shortest day of the year. Often in yoga, the solstice is celebrated by doing sun salutations. This simple form of sun salutation can be done with or without a yoga mat. It's an energizing and centering practice you can do anytime.

1. Stand with your feet hip-distance apart.
2. With an inhale, reach your arms overhead, and with your exhale, bring your hands to heart center. Inhale: arms overhead. Exhale: hands to heart center. You can repeat this simple flow three times or add a few extra steps:
3. Inhale: arms overhead. Exhale: hands to heart as you slowly bow into a forward fold.
4. Inhale for a halfway lift, bringing hands to your shins or thighs. Exhale: forward fold again.
5. With your next inhale, rise all the way to standing, and exhale hands back to heart. That's one round: repeat for three total rounds.

# 22

## DECEMBER

—

*I stand tall in the face of challenges and choose to view problems as opportunities for learning and expansion. I refuse to give up. In all that I do, I persevere.*

# 23

## DECEMBER

—

*I deserve good things, success, love, joy, and support in life. I am consistent, I am focused, and I've got this! It's not a matter of if, but when.*

# 24
## DECEMBER

### SEVEN SELFLESS ACTS OF SERVICE

A selfless act of service is something done with no ulterior motives or need for reciprocation. Performing a selfless act benefits both you and the person or people you're doing it for. A simple example is smiling at a stranger. Smiling at others can boost your mood while helping them feel more accepted and at ease. It's a win-win!

Commit to doing one act of service per day for the next week. Choose your own or use any of these examples:

- Smile at a stranger or offer someone a genuine compliment.
- Do volunteer work or donate old belongings you no longer use.
- Gift someone a book that positively impacted your life.
- Give a homeless person a bottle of water or hot coffee.
- Hold the door or elevator for someone.
- Let someone merge in front of you in traffic.
- Pick up any trash you see on the ground.

# 25

## DECEMBER

"You are allowed to be both a masterpiece and a work in progress, simultaneously."

**—SOPHIA BUSH**

# 26

## DECEMBER

*My peace and happiness do not rely on external factors. I am in charge of my feelings and how I choose to respond, rather than react.*

# 27

## DECEMBER

*I accept full responsibility for my life. I am responsible for my joy, my contentment, and my peace. Only I can give others permission to influence these aspects of me.*

# 28

___

## GUIDED VISUALIZATION

Your mind is incredibly powerful, and, combined with your thoughts, it is a key player in creating your reality. When you visualize something, your mind wants to paint the picture in its entirety.

Whether you're visualizing the life you want or a circumstance that worries you, your mind will fill that picture in with as much detail as possible, regardless of whether that vision is detrimental or advantageous. That's why it's important to focus your mind on what you want, down to the smallest detail. Put this into practice today with a guided visualization.

Need a pick-me-up? Guide your mind's eye through the detailed landscape of your happy place. Perhaps you choose to visualize reaching your highest goal in as much detail as possible. How would you feel? How would you act? Where would you be, and who would you be with? Home in on the details of your visualization.

# 29
## DECEMBER

*I am gracious and compassionate with myself because, like everyone else, I deserve to be treated this way. I am human and making mistakes is all part of the process!*

# 30
## DECEMBER

"Through your own transformation and embracing your magnificence, you will affect others around you in ways you may never fully understand. This is what changes the course of life. Yes, you are that wonderful."

**—FABIENNE FREDRICKSON**

# 31
## DECEMBER

———

*When I protect my peace, I remain calm, clear, and consistent. When I take time for myself, I feel at ease and a pervading sense of tranquility flows through me.*

# Resources

**BOOKS**

***Self Motivation Strategies for Women: How to Achieve Your Goals to Transform Every Aspect of Your Life*** by Jen Rulon (Rockridge Press, 2021)

***Self-Love Workbook for Women: Release Self-Doubt, Build Self-Compassion, and Embrace Who You Are*** by Megan Logan (Rockridge Press, 2020)

***The Self-Discovery Journal: 52 Weeks of Reflection, Inspiration, and Growth*** by Dr. Yana Lechtman (Rockridge Press, 2021)

**APP**

**Shine App:** www.theshineapp.com (access the Daily Shine Podcast from the app or search on Spotify)

**WEBSITE**

**YogiApproved.com:** www.yogiapproved.com (access the Mantra Mindset program free trial at www.yogiapproved.com/classes/mantra-mindset)

# References

Accad, Aila. *The Call of the Soul: A Path to Knowing Your True Self and Your Life's Purpose.* Weiser, 2013.

Adrain, Lorne A. *The Most Important Thing I Know: Life Lessons from Colin Powell, Stephen Covey, Maya Angelou, and Over 75 Other Eminent Individuals.* New York: MJF Books, 1999.

Ash, Mary Kay. "Her Wisdom." Mary Kay Tribute, n.d. marykaytribute.com /WisdomAttitude.aspx.

Barajas, Joshua. "Amanda Gorman's Poetic Answer to Pandemic Grief: 'Do Not Ignore the Pain.'" *PBS NewsHour.* January 21, 2021. pbs.org/new shour/arts/amanda-gormans-poetic-answer-to-pandemic-grief-do-not -ignore-the-pain.

BeBe, Izzie. *It's Complicated: A Love Story and Memoir.* Lulu Publishing Services, 2017.

Bhide, Sameer. *One Fine Day: Overcoming Adversity and Embracing the New Normal with Grace and Gratitude.* Bmb Publishing, 2020.

Blakely, Sara. "Top Five Startup Tips from Spanx Billionaire Sara Blakely." Interview by Clare O'Connor. *Forbes.* March 7, 2012. youtube.com /watch?v=Knjx4KsqBG4&t=59s.

Bowen, Will. *A Complaint Free World: How to Stop Complaining and Start Enjoying the Life You Always Wanted*. New York: Three Rivers Press, 2013.

Brown, Brené. *Rising Strong: How the Ability to Reset Transforms the Way We Live, Love, Parent, and Lead*. New York: Random House, 2017.

Brown, Brené. *The Gifts of Imperfection: Let Go of Who You Think You're Supposed to Be and Embrace Who You Are*. Random House Publishing Group, 2020.

Byrne, Rhonda. *The Secret*. New York: Atria Books, 2018.

Cade, Faith Broussard. fleurdelisspeaks. Instagram. n.d. instagram.com/p/CQUpCYMhi-y/.

Clements, Erin. "'Every Single Thing I Know, as of Today': Author Anne Lamott Shares Life Wisdom in Viral Facebook Post." TODAY.com. April 9, 2015. today.com/popculture/author-anne-lamott-shares-life-wisdom-viral-facebook-post-t13881.

Coelho, Paulo. *The Alchemist*. New York: HarperTorch, 2006.

Comăneci, Nadia. *Letters to a Young Gymnast*. New York: Basic Books, 2004.

Couric, Katie. "Find Out Who You Are and Live that Truth." *Glamour*. February 1, 2020. glamour.com/story/find-out-who-you-are-and-live-that-truth.

Covey, Stephen R., and James C. Collins. *The 7 Habits of Highly Effective People: Powerful Lessons in Personal Change*. New York: Simon & Schuster, 2020.

"Why Lalah Delia Is Urging Us All to Vibrate Higher Daily." Create & Cultivate. January 20, 2020. createcultivate.com/blog/health-wellness-lalah-delia -create-cultivate-100.

Cuddy, Amy. "Your Body Language May Shape Who You Are." *TED Talk.* Speech presented at the TEDGlobal 2012, June 2012.

Dreisbach, Shaun. "Simone Biles on How She Went from Foster Care to Olympic Gold." *Glamour.* November 1, 2016. glamour.com/story/women -of-the-year-simone-biles.

Du Châtelet, Émilie. *Selected Philosophical and Scientific Writings.* Edited by Judith P. Zinsser. Translated by Isabelle Bour and Judith P. Zinsser. Chicago: University of Chicago Press, 2009.

Engel, Amoryn. "A Night of Puffery and Huffington." *National Post* [Toronto, Canada]. June 9, 2007. newspapers.com/image/514228716/?terms =huffington&match=1.

ESPN.com News Services. "U.S. Soccer's Megan Rapinoe: I Wish 'I Knew That I Was Gay' Earlier." ESPN. August 5, 2016. espn.com/espnw/sports/story /_/id/17226931/uswnt-megan-rapinoe-says-wish-knew-was-gay -was-younger.

Francis, Deborah, and Hasheem Francis. *Built to Prosper for Women: The 9 Principles of Self-Mastery.* Plymouth, FL: BTP Publishing Group, 2016.

Fredrickson, Fabienne. *Embrace Your Magnificence: Get Out of Your Own Way and Live a Richer, Fuller, More Abundant Life.* Carlsbad, CA: Hay House, Inc., 2014.

Geurs, Karl, dir. *Pooh's Grand Adventure: The Search for Christopher Robin*. Written by Carter Crocker and Karl Geurs. Walt Disney Television Animation, 1997. VHS. Accessed via youtube.com/watch?v=9tRepZdoRmY&t=1s.

Hayes, Lisa M. "The Power of SelfTalk." *Lisa's Blog*. October 11, 2017. lisamhayes.com/blog/post/the-power-of-self-talk.

Kassem, Suzy. suzykassem.com/bknd/.

Keller, Helen. *We Bereaved*. Leslie Fulenwider, 1929.

Kent, Germany. *The Hope Handbook: The Search for Personal Growth*. Star Stone Press, 2015.

Knowles, Elizabeth, ed. *Little Oxford Dictionary of Proverbs*. Oxford University Press, 2009.

Lipsky-Karasz, Elisa. "Beyoncé's Baby Love." *Harper's Bazaar*. October 11, 2011. harpersbazaar.com/celebrity/latest/news/a825/beyonces-baby-love-interview-1111/.

Lo, Danica. "The Best Advice Ever from Madeleine Albright, Iman, Billie Jean King, and Serena Williams at Glamour's Women of the Year Awards." *Glamour*. November 9, 2015. glamour.com/story/best-advice-women-ever.

Lorde, Audre. *Sister Outsider: Essays and Speeches*. Berkeley, CA: Ten Speed Press, 2013.

Marcus, Bonnie. Bonnie Marcus Leadership, n.d. https://bonniemarcusleadership.com/.

Markle, Meghan. "'Suits' Star Meghan Markle Talks International Day of the Girl." *Breakfast Television*. Toronto, Canada: Citytv, October 7, 2015.

National Science Foundation. "Barbara McClintock." nsf.gov /news/special_reports/medalofscience50/mcclintock.jsp.

Nooyi, Indra. "The Best Advice I Ever Got." *Fortune*. April 30, 2008. archive .fortune.com/galleries/2008/fortune/0804/gallery.bestadvice.for tune/7.html.

Obama, Michelle. "Remarks by the First Lady during Keynote Address at Young African Women Leaders Forum." *The White House: President Barack Obama*. Speech presented at the Young African Women Leaders Forum, June 22, 2011. obamawhitehouse.archives.gov/the-press-office /2011/06/22/remarks-first-lady-during-keynote-address-young-african -women-leaders-fo.

Peale, Norman Vincent. *Positive Thinking Every Day: An Inspiration for Each Day of the Year*. New York: Fireside, 1993.

Perkins, Marion. "Who Is Amelia Earhart?" *Survey Graphic*. July 1, 1928.

Poehler, Amy. *Yes Please*. New York: Dey Street Books, 2014.

Rachel, T. Cole, and Lupita Nyong'o. "Lupita Nyong'o." *Interview*. November 5, 2013. interviewmagazine.com/film/lupita-nyongo.

Rawls, Alex. "Janelle Monáe: Being Unique May Make Others Uncomfortable." USA Today. July 4, 2014. usatoday.com/story/life/music/2014/07/04 /janelle-monae-prince-essence-music-festival-new-orleans/12215683/.

Rene, Zoe. *Your Mother Should Have Told You: A Girl's Guide to Being Good.* Bristol: SilverWood Books, 2015.

Retton, Mary Lou, and David Bender. *Mary Lou Retton's Gateways to Happiness: 7 Ways to a More Peaceful, More Prosperous, More Satisfying Life.* New York: Broadway Books, 2000.

Robbin, McKayla. *We Carry the Sky.* CreateSpace Independent Publishing Platform, 2016.

Roosevelt, Eleanor. *You Learn by Living: Eleven Keys for a More Fulfilling Life.* New York: Harper, 1960.

Rubin, Gretchen. *The Happiness Project, Tenth Anniversary Edition: Or, Why I Spent a Year Trying to Sing in the Morning, Clean My Closets, Fight Right, Read Aristotle, and Generally Have More Fun.* New York: HarperCollins Publishers, 2018.

Ruiz, Carolina. "Latinx Women in Medicine." American Medical Women's Association (AMWA). February 28, 2021. amwa-doc.org/latinx-women-in-medicine/.

Ruiz, Don Miguel. *The Four Agreements: A Practical Guide to Personal Freedom.* San Rafael, CA: Amber-Allen, 1997.

Ruth, Katrina. "7 Steps to Living Your Life With Purpose." *Entrepreneur.* July 18, 2019. https://www.entrepreneur.com/article/336600.

Schnall, Marianne, and Maya Angelou. "An Interview with Maya Angelou: Maya Angelou Talks about Her New Book." *Psychology Today.* February 17, 2009. psychologytoday.com/us/blog/the-guest-room/200902/interview-maya-angelou.

Simon, Samantha. "Suits Star Meghan Markle Shares 9 Tips for Ruling the Office." *InStyle*. Last modified July 9, 2015. https://www.instyle.com/news/suits-meghan-markle-tips-dressing-office.

Steinem, Gloria. *The Truth Will Set You Free, but First It Will Piss You Off: Thoughts on Life, Love, and Rebellion*. New York: Random House, 2019.

Tracy, Brian. *Eat That Frog!: 21 Great Ways to Stop Procrastinating and Get More Done in Less Time*. Berrett-Koehler Publishers, Inc., A BK Life Book, 2017.

Vanzant, Iyanla. *Faith in the Valley: Lessons for Women on the Journey to Peace*. New York: Atria Paperback, 2020.

Vanzant, Iyanla. "You Need to Work Your 'No' Muscle." SuperSoul Sessions, Oprah Winfrey Network (OWN). December 11, 2015. youtube.com/watch?v=KmxfWkDwN-4.

Weaver, Hilary, and Madison Feller. "Kamala Harris Reflects on Historic Win in First Speech as Vice President-Elect: 'I Will Not Be the Last.'" *Elle*. November 8, 2020. elle.com/culture/career-politics/a34607327/kamala-harris-speech-transcript-vice-president-election-2020/.

Winfrey, Oprah. *The Path Made Clear: Discovering Your Life's Direction and Purpose*. Bluebird, 2019.

Yousafzai, Malala. "Peter J. Gomes Humanitarian of the Year Award." Harvard Foundation. Speech presented at the Peter J. Gomes Humanitarian of the Year Award, 2013.

## ACKNOWLEDGMENTS

I would first and foremost like to thank the amazing team at Callisto Media for this opportunity. Immense gratitude to my husband, Tyler, for being my constant support every step of the way. A heartfelt thank-you to my family who checked on me and cheered me on, and my incredible community of friends who love and support me. Last, but certainly not least, *you*—the reader—who inspired me to write every single day. This writing process has been so enjoyable, and I come away feeling abundantly supported and grateful.

## ABOUT THE AUTHOR

**Ashton August** is the founder of the wellness website YogiApproved.com, an online yoga and fitness platform that plants a food-producing tree for every class a member completes, as well as an instructor for her YA classes. As a motivational author and speaker, distinguished yoga instructor, and wellness entrepreneur, she believes that cultivating empowering self-talk and a healthy mindset opens the door to living an abundantly fulfilling life! She lives in sunny Tucson, Arizona, with her husband and their two rescue dogs. She is also the author of *Learn, Grow, Shift: 30 Days of Personal Growth*. To learn more, visit AshtonAugust.com.

CPSIA information can be obtained
at www.ICGtesting.com
Printed in the USA
JSHW031544221221
21464JS00010B/365